The Totally Awesome

MONEY BOOK

FOR KIDS
(AND THEIR PARENTS)

ADRIANE G. BERG and

ARTHUR BERG BOCHNER

Newmarket Press

New York

This book is dedicated to Stuart Bochner,
a.k.a. Dad a.k.a. Stuart Spendthrift,
and thanks for thinking up the great games.

Copyright © 1993 Adriane G. Berg and Arthur Berg Bochner

This book published simultaneously in the United States of America and in Canada.

10 9 8

Library of Congress Cataloging-in-Publication Data

Berg, Adriane G.
      The totally awesome money book for kids (and their parents) / by Adriane G. Berg and Arthur Berg Bochner
            p.   cm.
      Includes bibliographical references and index.
      ISBN 1-55704-176-8 (pb)   ISBN 1-55704-183-0 (hc)
   1. Finance, Personal—Juvenile literature. 2. Budgets, Personal—Juvenile literature. [1. Finance, Personal.] I. Bochner, Arthur Berg . II. Title.
   HG173.8.B63   1993
   332.024—dc20   93-35812
                                                        CIP
                                                        AC

Quantity Purchases
Companies, professional groups, clubs, and other organizations may qualify for special terms when ordering quantities of this title. For information contact: Special Sales Department, Newmarket Press, 18 East 48th Street, New York, NY 10017, or call (212) 832-3575.

Book design by Deborah Daly

First edition

MANUFACTURED IN THE UNITED STATES OF AMERICA

Contents

A Word from Mom to Other Moms and Dads VII

Arthur's Introduction XII

Part 1
HOW TO MAKE YOUR IDEAS ABOUT MONEY GROW UP WITH YOU

1 MONEY: WHERE DOES IT COME FROM ANYWAY? **4**
$** The Mint **$ Counting All the Money in the United States **$** The Circulation of Money **$** Things You Can Do to Help Money Come Your Way

2 GOALS: WHAT DO YOU WANT FROM THE MONEY **12** IN YOUR LIFE?
$** Cheap and Expensive Goals **$ Turning a Wish into a Goal by Making a Plan **$** The Maze of Success

3 BUDGETS & SAVINGS: GREAT WAYS TO GET **19** THE STUFF YOU REALLY WANT
$** What Is a Budget? **$ How Come Some People Don't Use Budgets? **$** Balancing a Budget

4 BUDGETS: HOW TO GET MORE OF THOSE **25** GREAT SAVINGS
$** Two Types of Budgets—for Kids Who Are Spenders and Kids Who Are Savers **$ A Budget for Kids Who Like to Spend Money but Hate to Keep Track

5 MAKING THE MOST OF YOUR SAVINGS **30**
$** How to Make Saving Money Easier **$ Shopping for Interest Rates

Part 2
THE KIDS' GUIDE TO MAKING MONEY WITH THEIR MONEY

6 THE RISKS AND REWARDS OF MONEYMAKING   **36**

7 MAKING MONEY BY LENDING YOUR MONEY   **40**
TO OTHERS
$ Things to Know Before You Lend Your Money

8 SURPRISING ANSWERS TO THE QUESTION   **44**
"WHO WANTS TO BORROW A KID'S MONEY?"
$ The U.S. Government $ Cities and States $ Corporations $ Lending Your Money

9 MAKING MONEY: BUYING THINGS TODAY THAT   **51**
YOU CAN SELL FOR MORE MONEY TOMORROW
$ How to Pick the Right Stocks to Make Money $ For Kids Who Really Love Stocks $ How to Read the Financial Pages $ Arthur's Stock Tips

10 STOCKS: HOW TO INVEST MONEY YOU SAVE   **58**
FROM YOUR ALLOWANCE
$ Don't Be a DRIP: Buy One! $ Buying One Share

11 TOTALLY AWESOME: STOCK INVESTMENT   **62**
PLAN FOR KIDS USING MUTUAL FUNDS
$ Dollar Cost Averaging: How Any Kid Can Be a Great Investor

12 OTHER STUFF YOU CAN BUY TO MAKE A   **67**
PROFIT
$ Real Estate $ Commodities $ Collectibles

13 HOW TO SAVE THE PLANET   **71**

14 WHERE IN THE WORLD IS YOUR MONEY?   **74**
$ International Mutual Funds $ Other Ways to Make a
Profit in Foreign Countries $ Lending Money to the King
$ Currency: The Most Super Fun to Have with Money

15 BANKERS, BROKERS, FINANCIAL PLANNERS,   **79**
& OTHER MONEY EXPERTS
$ Bankers $ Brokers $ Financial Planners: New Kids
on the Block $ Real Estate Agents $ Insurance Sales-
men $ Lawyers, Accountants, and CPAs $ Read This
Before You Buy from a Broker

Part 3
CREDIT AND DEBT:
TWO SIDES OF THE SAME COIN

16 HOW EXPENSIVE IS MONEY TO BORROW?   **87**
$ How to Shop for Money $ The Plastic Flash: Credit
Cards $ Spend-and-Save Cards

17 BORROWING AND A KID'S FUTURE   **92**
$ When Borrowing Is No Good $ Totally Awesome
Ways of Borrowing Money $ Buying a House $ How
Leverage Makes You Money $ Leverage for Math Brains

Part 4
MONEY AND REAL LIFE

18 MONEY AND WORK   **101**
$ Get a Raise $ How Hard Is It for You to Ask for
Money or a Raise? $ A Word About Jobs $ What Would
You Do If…? $ A Word About Allowances

19 PAYING BILLS   **109**
$ How to Balance a Checkbook

Part 5
MONEY MATTERS FOR OLDER KIDS

20 GETTING TO COLLEGE   **115**
$ Don't Let the Numbers Scare You $ My Top Five Best Bets for Getting to College $ What to Do With the Money Your Parents Saved for College

21 NOW THAT YOU HAVE MADE SOME MONEY,   **119** IT'S TIME TO PAY YOUR TAXES
$ The U.S. Government's Totally Awesome Tax System $ How Much Tax Will You Pay? $ Investing to Save Taxes $ The Kiddie Tax: No Kidding

FINAL NOTE: HOW YOU FEEL ABOUT MONEY   **124** SAYS A LOT ABOUT YOU
$ Goals: What Are Yours? $ Do You Have a Plan to Reach Your Goals? $ Budgets: A Look at Thomas $ Money in Your Future $ What Do You Consider Financial Success? $ Collector, Trader, or Buyer—Which Are You? $ Socially Responsible Investing: What Do You Believe In? $ Taxes: Do You Think They Are Fair?

HEY, KIDS, THIS PART IS JUST BETWEEN   **128** YOU AND ME

MOM GETS THE LAST WORD   **131**
$ How to Discuss Family Money Culture $ Family Financial Tree

Glossary   **134**

Bibliography   **139**

Index (including Game List)   **141**

The buck
starts here.

A Word from Mom
to Other Moms and Dads

How happy are you with the way you handle money? You'd be a major exception if you were satisfied with your money skills. In my work as a lawyer, author, estate planner, and broadcaster in personal finance I know that knowledge is not enough. Confidence, familiarity, and perspective are far more important, and they are harder to learn in adulthood.

Last week, I spoke at the Plaza Hotel in New York City to an audience of several hundred multimillionaires from as far away as Ontario. I told them how to invest their money. The evening was a great success and ended with applause. There wasn't a nervous bone in my body.

Next Tuesday, I am scheduled to meet with my broker to instruct him on how to invest my children's college funds and my own paltry pension. I can hardly swallow. As author of eight books on personal finance and host of the "Money Show" on WABC, I have all the tools I need to be a financial information machine. But that's not enough. There is such a thing as "financial poise." Like any other coping skill, it comes from feelings of competence and mastery best learned in childhood.

For the most part, if we want our children to be confident about money handling, including investing and credit, we are going to have to teach them ourselves. Although times are changing slowly, the plain fact is that financial decision making is not taught in school, is not often taught at home, and does not come naturally. The result for most of us is lifelong anxiety and sometimes disastrous mistakes over money management.

Despite the tough economic times, it is still possible to earn money in America; but it's getting harder to invest and preserve what you've earned. For our kids, it will be harder still. Like you, I want my children—Arthur, age eleven (my coauthor), and Rose, age two—to have a familiarity with money that I never had growing up. When my friends and I look back on things, we agree that our ignorance about money matters was more of a handicap than a lack of inheritance or limited earning capacity. It just takes too long to catch up when you don't begin to grasp the basics until you've already worked for several years.

In my book *Your Wealthbuilding Years,* I emphasized the importance of early planning to those eighteen and older. But there is an even better time to start. How about fifth grade! I wish that my folks or my school or both would have paid as much attention to developing my money skills as they did to developing my social skills.

Of course, when I was a kid, Columbus was packing for his first sail. So you'd think that by now things would be different. The schools are trying, and my publisher hopes to share this book with many schools. There are some wonderful inroads being made in schools, but they are certainly not reaching every student.

My son, Arthur, for example, is a student at a very typical suburban public school. Aside from his academic studies, he has two required special courses: Health Education and Home Economics.

In the former, he learns about cholesterol, free radicals, and food allergies, and, of course, sex. At age eleven, he's not expected to have a heart attack or a baby. Still, the school sees fit to help him avoid having either too soon; it's considered part of his education for the future. Yet, not one word is spoken to prepare him to spend, save, or invest the money he will inevitably earn.

In Home Economics, a weekly session teaches the kids self-esteem, assertiveness, and drug avoidance. The kids talk about handling sibling rivalry, teasing, and cheats. Yet, even in this innovative curriculum, money training is completely absent.

There is a growing recognition for the need, but only a very few children are lucky enough to receive any basic training in money matters through their school.

At least for now, teaching my children about the buck stops and starts with me. So I include Arthur in many financial discussions, both about our own family and about money in general. Because it's my field, I have tools unavailable to most—books, software, even board games.

For the past two years I volunteered to lecture at a children's business camp sponsored by The Foundation for Free Enterprise, part of the New Jersey State Chamber of Commerce. It was quite an experience, preparing fifteen-year-olds to manage their money and to contribute to a pension plan that wouldn't exist for almost ten more years. They had trouble grasping the concept of retirement, were used to relying on their parents for money, and were already using credit cards! But the effort paid off. The kids loved the material and absorbed it all.

As for Arthur, he understands financial fundamentals and is well on his way to being a money mogul. I don't want you to get the wrong idea. Arthur has no intention of making money his life or his life's work. At the moment, he wants to be a paleobotanist because he just saw *Jurassic Park*. In fact, one of the great gifts I believe he has is that he is not obsessive about money; he is able to keep it in perspective. He's comfortable making a decision, acting on it, and forgetting about it.

It goes without saying (I think) that I know much more about money than Arthur. I'm the expert and I've got thirty-four years on him. But he has one big advantage: His comfort level is very high.

When Arthur selects a stock, I have to place the order because he is too young to control his own account. I'm always a little worried about making a trade. Self-confidence comes after knowledge and not always as fast. But Arthur is a cool customer. And I can see that this emotional advantage when it comes to money is something valuable to cultivate in a child.

His feeling of security about money makes him very generous. He shares, is not stingy, and has a healthy optimistic attitude about the future. I see no moral downside in teaching kids about money.

I hope that one day this book will be looked at the way we regard the Edison Cylindar, an ancient artifact that started something that is always developing and improving. I looked everywhere but could find no book for children that taught basic economics, global investing, stock selection, credit use, and socially responsible investing at their level.

Words such as *leverage, price/earnings ratio, interest,* and *cred-*

itworthy can be understood before age thirty. Other concepts that many grown-ups still find difficult, such as mutual fund investing, dollar cost averaging, and American Depository Receipts, are absorbed by kids if they are not made into a big deal.

Kids' attention span, memory, and tolerance for learning new things are much sharper than ours. They are good at processing new ideas—better than we are. On the other hand, they have no experience of the world. They have never been fired, needed to pay for a necessity, or been faced with a week off from work without vacation pay.

Most don't know what things cost. My fifteen-year-old students and my son and his adolescent friends remind me of Dustin Hoffman's character in *Rainman;* they can do the heaviest math but may not know the difference in cost between a house and a car.

We are going to have to be sensitive to the uneven manner in which money matters are learned. Your kids will grasp some things surprisingly quickly; you'll think you've uncovered a miniature Bernard Baruch. Then you will discover that he or she thinks a mailman earns $1 million a year.

That's why, in this book, you will find complex material that may be new to you side by side with a matching game or story. There is no way I could have written this book without Arthur. So when my publisher asked me to write a "prequel" to *Your Wealthbuilding Years,* I took Arthur on as a sidekick. But I was in for a surprise. The book ended up being his! We worked together with our word processor on. Sometimes Arthur wrote an entire chapter and I reviewed it. Other times I engineered the ideas, made sure he understood, and could apply what I was saying. Often I showed him a real-life example of the material. For example, in the tax chapter he learned about withholding. He understood the concept; but only when I showed him my pay stub did the horrible reality of taxation set in. If you can't tell who wrote what as you read the book, join the club; neither can we. That means that a lot of this book, for all practical purposes, was ultimately written by an eleven-year-old.

That fact proved to me that at least some of my techniques work. For example, very hard concepts such as the money supply, inflation, investing, and stock analysis are presented casually. There is no feeling that the material is too hard or just for special kids. It's no big deal. Kids should know reading, writing, arithmetic, and the price/earnings ratio of stocks.

Although most parents do give kids an allowance on a regular basis, let's face it, in this economy neither you nor I can give our kids all the money we would wish. And having seen so many troubled rich kids, I'm not so sure that the silver spoon is such a wonderful utensil. But knowledge and courage about money can do a child a lot of good as he or she matures.

I don't expect kids to go out and buy a government bond at age twelve or start a pension plan at age fifteen, although this book teaches them how to do both. But they learn health education and sex education for their future, so why not money education, too?

We can join together to teach this without nagging and without compromising our values. Here are some things I learned that will make it easier for you to help your kids along with this book:

$ Kids have a different sense of time in relation to money. Concepts in the faraway future, such as retirement, are hard to grasp emotionally. So when explaining things such as savings, talk about immediate goals because kids live in the present. Teenagers have a great deal to cope with right now. They are not meant to dwell on aging.

$ To kids, wealth comes from love, not from net worth. This sounds corny, but it's true. When Arthur's friends describe rich and poor, the rich always have a loving family, are neat, and eat together. Arthur's friends seldom pick the families that I would usually target as rich, the ones with big houses and big cars. So explain security and prosperity rather than wealth and riches.

$ Some kids worry about money. Some kids worry when they learn about mortgages and collateral. They may be scared that the house they live in doesn't belong to them. Be aware that kids think deeply and that they need reassurance about money.

$ Kids like money and know more about it than you imagine. Kids like the feel of change in their pockets. They like to have control and pick what they want at a store. If you say no, they whine. If they are in control, they are often frugal savers. Go figure!

Arthur's ideas on what he wanted to include in this book and how he wanted the material presented were a source of constant wonderment to me. The choices were surprisingly varied—some basic, some sophisticated.

But so is the knowledge of the ten-to-teen, no longer a baby and not yet an adult. I went with the flow of Arthur's level of understanding, and I believe it will parallel that of your kids. Have fun!

Arthur's Introduction

> *"I have no money.
> I'm just a kid."*
> —Shortsighted Sam

I know what you're thinking: "I have no money. I'm just a kid. So why do I have to know all this money stuff?" Well, that's what I thought, too, until I found out all the benefits I get from knowing about money.

Even though I don't have much now, I found out that a person earning the minimum wage of $4.25 an hour and working a regular work week from age twenty-five to sixty-five will earn $250,000. That's a quarter of a million dollars. I can't even think that high. But that's the minimum amount of money you and I will handle in the years to come. Wow!

I also learned that my parents, who still don't let me make my own decisions about spending, give me permission a lot easier because I pay attention to prices and costs.

Sometimes when they talk (or fight) about money, it's easier on me because I understand what's going on. How about you? When your parents talk about money, do you sometimes not understand it and feel bad? After reading this book, you might feel better about it. You might even be allowed to take part in the conversation.

This book gives you a head start in life by making you money wise. It includes subjects such as borrowing, working, and even taxes. If you read this book, you will have a basic understanding of money. Key terms, called Moneytalk, are explained throughout the book.

You will find out how to use a budget to help you save your money. You will learn what goals are and how to reach them. You will learn about savings and what they can do for you.

You can also use this information to amass a small fortune. And in other parts of the book, you will find ways to amass a large fortune through investing and lending.

Also, I think money know-how is important to help us make a difference in the world. So you will find a chapter on how to use money responsibly to encourage a better environment and other things about which we care.

My philosophy is that money is around the corner if you are looking for it. You may be able to find it easier after you read this book.

Find the Money

Circle the words, listed in the column on the left, that you can find forwards and backwards, up or down. Then look for the money. Turn the page for the answer.

	P	L	T	Q	M	A	S
Schools	R	E	H	C	A	E	T
Magic	U	L	G	B	G	Z	G
Bright	L	X	I	C	I	U	Y
Teacher	E	P	R	L	C	U	M
Rules	S	U	B	J	E	C	T
Zeros	A	C	Z	H	S	M	E
Choose	N	P	E	R	O	H	R
Subject	I	U	R	M	O	J	M
Terms	S	L	O	O	H	C	S
	C	X	S	Z	C	O	W

Answer:

It's a Dollar Sign = $

```
      T       M
R  E  H  C  A  E  T
   U  G     G
   L  I     I
   E  R     C
S  U  B  J  E  C  T
   Z     S     T
   E     O     E
   R     O     R
S  L  O  O  H  C  S
   S     C
```

Part 1

How to Make Your Ideas About Money Grow Up with You

You already know a lot more about money than you think or than some grown-ups realize. Most of you buy a school lunch and know the price. Some of you already have had a job, others get an allowance, and some of you have even made investments.

Maybe you got a gift from your grandparents and wanted to spend it on a toy or game. Your folks had you put it away for savings instead. Even little babies get piggy banks and some change as a nursery toy. All the popular TV and cartoon characters have money-related toys to sell. Sesame Street, Disney, and Barney merchandise companies make "character banks." Maybe you own one.

Not only do you know something about saving and spending, but if you are like most kids, you are an aware consumer, too. On the back of your cereal box there may be a coupon to get money back. Your town may have a law that requires a deposit on soda cans and bottles and gives a refund when they are returned. Maybe you already look for sales or buy toys at flea markets.

Your parents may talk about money in the home, to you or each other. There may be talks, discussions, even fights about money taking place around you. If you or your older brother or sister is near college age, the cost of school is surely a topic of conversation.

As you grow up, money will take on a bigger role in your life. Someday you will be the mom or dad who supports the family, makes the money decisions, and keeps everyone in the food, clothing, and shelter they need.

It's important that as you grow up, the ideas you have about money grow up with you. One babyish thing that stops many grown-ups from feeling comfortable with money is the idea that to be good with money you must be good with math. Money has nothing to do with math, whether you like math or not. Many grown-ups shy away from money management because they don't think they are good in math. Their money habits didn't mature with them.

While it's important to know how to add and subtract, you can get the idea of how money works in your life without being a math genius. To give you a better head start than most grown-ups have, Part I gives you a grasp of where your money comes from now and later, shows you the importance of setting goals, and even begins you on a budget and savings plan.

And you can learn and do all this even if you're not handling any money now. Did your mom or dad ever buy you clothes a little too big so you could wear them for a long time while you grew? Well, this book is like that. Some of the ideas are a little too big for some of you to use right now. But, for sure, you will grow into them. It will be good that you already have the tools you need when the time comes. In that way, your ideas about money will grow as you do.

1 Money: Where Does It Come From Anyway?

When you find a penny on the street or you watch your mom pay for something at the store, do you ever wonder where the money comes from? Why are these coins and paper the things we use to trade for the stuff we want? How do we get money and keep it? How come some people have more money than others have?

The Mint

Believe it or not, each country, including the United States, makes its own money. The factory where our money is manufactured is called the *mint*. It's located in Washington, D.C., and you and your folks can visit it any weekday for free.

If you do, you'll see how coins are cast and paper money

is printed. You will also see how old bills are destroyed. There are heavy security checks to make sure no one takes any of the newly minted money or the old money slated for destruction.

Counting All the Money in the United States

Our own government, mostly through an agency called the *Fed* (short for *Federal Reserve Board*), makes the decision about how much money to manufacture. The people who work for the Fed, such as the Chief Economist, take a count of all the money in circulation. They check out how much is in bank accounts and other places where people like your parents keep their money. They check out how banks are lending money and whether it's easy or hard to get money.

Economists at work

They add up all the money out there and call the total *M-1*. If M-1 is low, they can actually print more money or do other things to encourage banks to lend money and you to borrow. If there is too much money out there, sometimes prices go up. Maybe you know the word *inflation*. That means things are getting too expensive because there is a lot of money around and people will pay high prices. When that happens, the Fed can make the money supply tighter.

In our country, we each control the money in coins and paper that comes our way. The more of it we keep, the more wealthy we are. The less we have, the less wealthy. So far, we are the wealthiest country in the whole world. But, remember, wealth comes from three things: getting money in the first place, keeping the money in the second place, and making the money grow in the third place.

Money Juggler

As you get older, you will get better at doing all three. Kids like to think that the hardest part is getting the money in the first place. I can't remember getting any money until I was nine. And then I got it only because I collected my

father's change. I used to just ask my parents for stuff.
Sometimes I got it, and sometimes I didn't.

In the last two years, I really learned a lot about where
money comes from and how to keep it and make it grow.
Here are all the places I can think of where people, even
kids, can get money. Can you think of any more?

$ Earn it at job such as delivering groceries or news-
papers.
$ Earn it in a business such as a lemonade stand.
$ Trade for it with something you have, like a base-
ball card.
$ Find it in the street.
$ Win it in a game.
$ Get a gift of money.
$ Get a scholarship or an award for doing something
well.
$ Get a refund or a rebate for bringing something
back to a store like soda bottles or cans.

If we keep any of this money that comes our way in a
bank, it's also counted as part of the nation's money supply.
So my bank account is part of M-1—awesome.

Actually all our money is connected. If there is lots of it,
people spend. If they spend, business does well. If business
does well, more people have jobs. They then have more
money to spend. In Moneytalk, this is called a *recovery* or
an *expansion*.

It goes the other way, too. With less money around, there
is less spending, less business and fewer jobs. This is called
a *recession*. My mom says that she has lived through eight
recessions since 1954. That shows that the economy
changes. It goes in cycles, and we must realize that times
change for good and bad and be prepared for both.

THE M-1 POEM

There was an old Fed
With money to spread
Who made an old banker a loan.
Along came a man
With a big moving van
And was able to buy an old home.
He needed some paint
So his wife wouldn't faint,
So he hired a boy with a brush.
When I pay you today,
put the money away.
You'll increase the M-I in a rush.

The Circulation of Money

Money has two sides, just like a coin. Think of money as heads and tails. Heads you earn; tails you spend. But the weird part about it is that every time you spend, another person earns what you spent.

When you buy a juice box for 50 cents, you pay the storekeeper with the money you spent for it. You spent; he earned. Then, when the storekeeper wants to buy something for himself, he will spend your 50 cents. The person he buys from will earn it. This shows us how money stays in circulation all the time.

Money keeps moving in a healthy economy. When people get afraid to spend because they are afraid they won't earn, everything breaks down and we have a recession.

The Heads and Tails Money Game

Play this simple game and you will see for yourself:
Give each player 5 pennies. Make one team Heads and the other

team Tails. Flip a quarter. If it lands on heads, the Heads team gets a penny from the Tails team. If it lands on tails, the Tails team gets a penny from the Heads team. Keep track of how many times you can play before all the coins are earned by one team.

The tossing of the coin can result in one team winning with as few as five tosses. More likely, it will take as many as 25 or even 50 tosses before one team wins. It can go on forever, with an infinite number of tosses. A game with a lot of tosses is like a healthy national economy. Things stay moving. The same currency (money) is spent and respent by all the people.

The grand total of all the money spent and respent from what is made to be sold is our *gross national product (GNP)*. It is a good measure of the wealth of our country. If people stop spending, other people stop making things to spend on. The GNP gets smaller, and the country gets poorer. It's like a quick game where one side got all the pennies fast and the game stopped—no fun.

But even in a slow economy, some people have enough money. That's because they know how to do some extra things to help the money come their way.

Things You Can Do to Help Money Come Your Way

Money won't come to you in all the ways I've mentioned all the time, but I've found that it helps to be on the lookout. My friends are all very different types when it comes to money. Some think about it; some don't. Some try to learn about money, and some find it boring. It doesn't matter; they're all great kids. But I did notice one thing: The kids who pay attention to money stuff seem to have more.

Here are some of the things my friends do to have money come their way:

- $ Take soda cans back to the store to get a 5 cent refund.
- $ Work. (A girl I know is an actress, and a boy I know gives tennis lessons to younger kids; others have paper routes and mow lawns.)
- $ Start a business. (That's me; right now, I sell dinosaurs at flea markets to cash in on the *Jurassic Park* craze.)
- $ Pick up a penny. (I once saw a "Candid Camera" show where no one even bothered to pick up a dime they saw on the street. I guess it didn't mean much to the grown-ups. My friends would pick it up. Would you?)
- $ Ask for money. (For sure, I don't have all the stuff I want. But lots of what I like is expensive, like a chess set. So my grandparents can't buy it for me as a gift. Lately, when they ask what I want for my birthday, I say money to save up for something big.)

Eventually, we will all work, and money will come our way. The trouble is that money comes, but it also goes. Sometimes money gets spent so fast that grown-ups have to start all over every week from scratch. So it doesn't matter how much comes their way; they never get any wealth.

But the good thing about money is that even when it goes, it can come back and stay awhile. There was a boy named Abe. His parents had very little money come their way. So Abe decided to work hard and put himself through school. He became a lawyer. He learned how to make his money grow. Eventually, he got an important job and stayed wealthy. That boy was Abraham Lincoln.

A boy named George was also poor. His parents put him in an orphanage. He became an athlete and made even more money than the President of the United States. But he didn't know how to keep that money. Pretty soon, there wasn't much left. George's middle name was Herman, but everyone called him Babe—Babe Ruth.

The point is that people aren't just rich or poor. Money doesn't stay away or stay put. You control what happens to the money that comes your way. You can start right now by paying attention to how much money you have and figure out where it comes from. Add up how much money you have, and where it comes from. Add up how much you have today. Is it $.25, $25.00, or even more? However much it is, the money is yours. It does what you want it to do. That's why goals are so important, even to us kids. Let's look at goals in the next chapter.

THE MONEY I HAVE NOW (also called your *gross assets*— how's that for Moneytalk?):

Amount   I got it from

_____Gift

_____Allowance

_____Found it

_____Earned it

_____Won it

_____Refund

_____Rebate

_____Return on an investment

2
Goals: What Do You Want from the Money in Your Life?

"If you know exactly what you want, you're halfway to getting it."
—Gail Goalsetter

A *goal* is something that you want for yourself or someone you love; it's a target, a thing you want to achieve. Anything from the toys you would like to own to the college you would like to attend can be a goal. Money is useful to meet your goals. Sometimes, all you need is the money, like when your goal is to go to a movie. Other times, money is only part of a goal, like when you want to start a business.

So to get what you really want from the money in your life, it's important to set goals and know how much they cost. When you do this, here are some of the good things that happen:

- $ You don't waste money on things you don't want.
- $ You can give up the things that are less important to get the things that are more important.

$ You can go on to the next goal when you reach
  your first goal.
$ You are happy even if you are working hard,
  because you anticipate the reward you will get.

Cheap and Expensive Goals

There are two types of goals: things that you want right
away and things that are for the future. In Moneytalk, the
ones you want now are called *short-term* goals. The future
ones are called *long-term* goals.

Some long-term goals are college, retirement, buying a
house, opening a business. Some short-term goals are going
to the movies, buying a bike, Christmas gifts for the family,
or money for a school trip. Most long-term goals, such as
college, cost a lot of money. But so do some short-term
goals. Many teenagers want a car right away. It's a short-
term goal, but it's expensive. Still, short-term goals are usually cheaper and faster to save for than the long-term goals.

Sometimes, you must give up short-term goals to reach
your long-term goals. No one I know gets all the short- and
long-term goals they want, but there is a way to get many of
them. The way is by making a *plan*.

Turning a Wish into a Goal by Making a Plan

When I first thought about my goals, long term and short
term, they were just a bunch of wishes. But if I made a plan
to reach them, I could turn a wish into a goal that I could
achieve.

Here are some short-term goals:

$ Getting a Mickey Mantle rookie card
$ Getting a Super Nintendo Entertainment System

$ Buying a remote-control car
$ Getting a Compact Disc player
$ Buying a box of Fleer Ultra baseball cards

Here are some long-term goals:

$ College
$ Being a lawyer
$ Getting married
$ Buying an apartment
$ Retiring at sixty

So, the first money basic is:

List your wishes; then make a plan. A plan turns a wish into a goal that you are able to achieve.

List some of your wishes now. After reading the chapter on budgets (Chapter 3), you'll see how you can reach them by setting goals and making a plan.

My wishes are:

My goals are:

My plans are:

Here's a quiz to see if you know the difference between a wish, a goal, and a plan. Put *G* for goal, *W* for wish, and *P* for plan:

1. Owning all the video games in the store
2. Saving to buy a video game
3. Owning Super Mario Bros. 3

1. Going to college
2. Working to pay for college
3. Getting all A's at college

1. Buying a tie for Dad
2. Buying Dad a present
3. Finding a men's clothing sale

Remember the difference between goals, plans, and wishes. A goal is your target, the thing you want. A plan is the way you intend to reach your goal and get what you want. A wish is something you want, but have no plan to get. Without a plan, wishes often don't come true. With a plan, a wish becomes a goal in your control.

When what you want is almost impossible or very unnecessary, it's probably just a wish (owning all the video games in the store). When you know exactly what you want, you have a goal (owning Super Mario Bros. 3). When you know what you must do to get it, you have a plan (saving).

Some things are wishes that can become goals. Getting all A's in college is a wish. But once you get there, you can make it a goal by having a study program.

"Be careful what you wish for, you might get it! Don't save for a puppy or a scuba outfit if you really won't use it or care for it."
—Pablo Payment

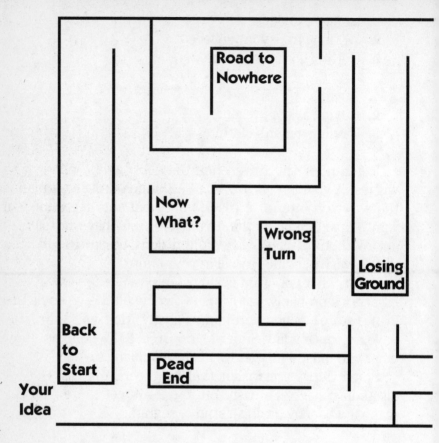

Some things are just wishes because they are not clear enough in your mind (buying Dad a present). If they get clear, they are goals (buying a tie for Dad).

As you keep reading this book, come back to this chapter and add wishes, plans, and goals. Maybe you have already reached some of your goals. Make a list of them right now.

Goals I already made:

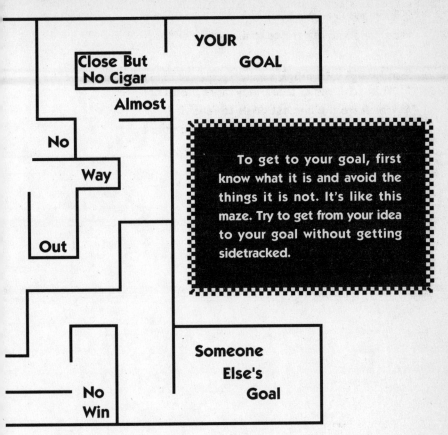

To get to your goal, first know what it is and avoid the things it is not. It's like this maze. Try to get from your idea to your goal without getting sidetracked.

No matter how old you are now, you will always have new goals all your life. And you will always have to make new plans. So the sooner you get used to it, the better.

The Maze of Success

From now on, instead of thinking you can have everything or can't have anything, make plans for the things that are really important and stick with them. One type of plan that involves money is a savings plan. We'll talk about this in the next chapter.

Things to Do

Here are some questions to ask your parents:

$ What are their goals?

$ What achievements are they most proud of?

$ Which are the hardest goals to reach?

$ What were their goals when they were your age?

3
Budgets and Savings:
Great Ways to Get the Stuff You Really Want

"Budgets are for everyone. No one has too little or too much money to make a budget."

What Is a Budget

A *budget* is a way of keeping track of the money you get and the money you spend. When you know how much things cost and how you are spending your money, lots of good things happen.

For example, if you know that candy costs 50 cents at the drugstore, you won't pay 75 cents to a candy machine. Also, by having an idea of how much you have to spend, you won't fall into the trap of overspending. With a budget, you won't use up your allowance by the middle of the week and have to ask for more money or go without the stuff you want.

But the super thing about a budget is that it helps you get all the things you really want. It shows you how much of your money is spent on junk you don't need or want. Finally, a budget helps you save for the expensive things that you can't afford to buy right away.

How Come Some People Don't Use Budgets?

Some people give budgets a bad rap because they think that budgeting makes you give up the things that make you happy. They think that a budget is like a diet, where you have to stop yourself from having fun. Just the opposite is true. Let's look at what happened when a boy named Thomas made a budget and how he got everything he wanted.

THOMAS'S TOTALLY AWESOME BUDGET

Thomas is fourteen years old, and he was always running out of money. There was a long list of stuff he wanted and couldn't have. He often got into trouble because of this. For example, one day he spent the class trip money his father gave him on extra candy. Then he sold his favorite baseball card in order to make the trip money back. Thomas didn't enjoy the candy, missed his baseball card, and was miserable during the class trip. Can this boy be saved? *Yes. With a budget!*

To make a budget, the first thing you should do is write down all the money that you get from anyone, in any form. All gifts, allowance, and payments for work are included. Don't bother with money you find only once in a while. You can't count on that every week. All this incoming money is called *income* in Moneytalk.

Here is Thomas's income:

$ $3.00 a day school lunch money
  (5 days x $3.00) $15.00
$ $10.00 a week allowance every Saturday $10.00
$ $5.00 a week for mowing Mr. Willis's lawn $ 5.00

If we add this all up, we find that Thomas's income each week is $30.00. When Thomas did the math, he was shocked at how much income he had. It was even more puzzling that he never had enough money. This was because Thomas didn't keep track of his spending.

Next, you should write down all the things you spend on. This is what living costs you. It's called the *cost of living* or your *expenses*. When Thomas did the second part of the budget, the mystery was solved.

Here are Thomas's expenses:

$ $3.50 a day for school lunch (The price of the school lunch went up by 50 cents; but Thomas never paid any attention, so he never told his parents that the price increased.)

$ $2.50 a day for after-school snack (Every day because his friend Jim ordered the special, Thomas bought the special at the pizzeria. It was two slices and a soda for $2.50. Thomas only ate one slice and threw the other one away. That means that Thomas spent all his after-school snack and mowing money on something he threw away each day.)

And now it is time to take a third step, the list that most people who make budgets forget to do. Thomas was ready to make a list of the things he really wanted.

Thomas wanted:

$ A puppy
$ Another Nintendo game
$ Pump sneakers

"Wow," thought Thomas, "I'll never get that stuff." He realized that he spent his extra money on gum, baseball

How Do You Feel?

How do you feel when other kids have more money to spend than you? Does it make a difference if they are your close friends? If so, why? Other kids have less money to spend than you? Does it make a difference if they are your close friends? If so, why?

cards, plastic charms, and other cheap stuff because what he really wanted was so expensive he never believed he could get it. Without a budget, he would have just spent his money on quick substitutes for his real dreams.

With his budget, look what Thomas did:

He told his parents that the price of a school lunch had increased. They gave him the extra 50 cents each day. Next, he stopped buying the pizza special. Instead, he bought one slice for $1.50 and took an extra juice from home. Making those changes saved Thomas $7.50 a week, and he and Jim are still pals.

Thomas started to concentrate on the things he really wanted. After getting permission from his parents, he got a free puppy from the dog pound! The manager asked for a $7.50 fee for the dog's shots. Thomas's parents were surprised when he had the money. Also, Thomas told everyone he knew about the Nintendo game he wanted and asked if they knew where to buy one at a low price. Within a week, a girl named Judy offered to trade her game in return for some baseball cards plus $14.00 in cash.

It was a fair deal for both of them. Instead of spending $50.00 on a new game, Thomas spent $14.00 and traded some of his duplicate cards. Judy got rid of a game she was tired of and got some money and cards she really wanted.

Finally, the pump shoes were the only thing left on

Thomas's most-wanted list. Thomas's income was $32.50 a week. But his expenses were much less. Lunch and snacks cost him $25.00 a week. With the extra money, Thomas decided to save $7.50 a week for the sneakers. It took him 10 weeks to buy the sneakers, but he enjoyed wearing them very much.

Balancing a Budget

Budgeting is like playing on a teeter-totter. It should balance on both sides. Cutting down on expenses can be just as helpful as adding money.

The Teeter-Totter Riddle

Try this balancing feat:

Four friends are playing on the teeter-totter. John weighs 90 pounds and Mary 60 pounds, for a total of 150 pounds on the right side. Leroy weighs 80 pounds and David 70; they balance the left side at 150 pounds.

Now rearrange the friends when Jesus, who weighs 40 pounds, wants to play. Can you do it?

Just put Leroy and John together and David, Mary, and Jesus on the other side for balance. Each side is now 170 pounds, and they balance.

NOW BALANCE YOUR OWN BUDGET

Here are some things you should include in your budget.

List your income:

- $ Weekly allowance
- $ Lunch money
- $ Job 1
- $ Job 2
- $ Other

- $ Once in a while
- $ Gifts
- $ Bonus
- $ Other

List your expenses:

$ Food $ Toys
$ Transportation $ Clothes
$ School trips $ Gifts for others
$ Snacks $ Other

Take your income and subtract your expenses. Are you over or under your budget? Or are you even?

If you are under budget, save that extra money. If there is none, start a plan to spend less and add savings to your weekly income.

America's Annual Budget
_____

$ Housing=$8,078
$ Food and drink= $4,017
$ Clothing=$1,489
$ Transportation= $5,093
$ Medical costs=$1,298
$ Social Security tax and savings= $1,935
$ Other= $3,982

This is the budget for a family that earns $28,540. Add up the expenses, and deduct them from the income. What's left over is what the family can save. (These numbers come from 1988 Bureau of Labor Statistics publications.)

4
Budgets: How to Get More of Those Great Savings

> *"The best way to get more money to spend on the things you want is to make a budget for the money you have."*
>
> —Responsible Rhoda

If you think about Thomas's story, you'll see how many things he learned from budgeting. Here are a few things you can learn about your own money with a budget:

$ How much income are you getting? Where does it come from? How can you increase it?

$ Where is your money going? Can you get the same things cheaper? Are the things worth the money? Are you getting what you really want?

$ What do you really want? Can you get it for free? Can you borrow it? Trade for it?

$ How long will it take to save for it?

Above all, Thomas learned that budgets are a personal thing. What stuff you want is up to you and your parents.

He didn't have to eat what Jim ate, and he didn't have to want what Judy wanted. And if you want to be like everyone else, that's OK, too. When you save with a budget, you are not stopping yourself from getting what you want. Just the opposite. You are taking control of your money so you can get what you want.

Two Types of Budgets—for Kids Who Are Spenders and Kids Who Are Savers

PENELOPE AND STEVEN GO TO THE TOY STORE

Penelope Pennypincher and Steven Spender go to the toy store.

Each has $10.00 to spend. They look around. Penelope says, "I like this game, but it costs $4.95. That's too expensive. I've seen it for $4.00 in another store. I won't spend this much." Steven says, "You're silly. Why wait? Is it worth saving 95 cents and miss out on playing the game this afernoon? Anyway, I like this game that costs $9.99. Since I have $10.00, I'm going to buy it.

"Now hurry up and pick something," says Steven. But Penelope leaves the store without buying anything. Penelope has the whole $10.00 left and no game. Steven has a game and a penny left.

Which of these kids is more like you? Was there a right or wrong attitude? Which of them would you rather know and feel comfortable with?

Some kids like to keep records and put down everything they get and spend. Others don't like to. They forget or get bored. Still, everyone needs to have a budget. If you are the kind of kid who likes to keep track of money, use the form at the end of Chapter 3 every month. Each day, keep a record of income and expenses to enter on your budget form.

A Budget for Kids Who Like to Spend Money but Hate to Keep Track

"I say, 'A penny saved is a penny earned.' Steven Spender says, 'Live for today—tomorrow will take care of itself.' What do you say?"

—Penelope Pennypincher

If you don't like all that pencil and paper action, there is a special trick. Even if you are a kid who likes to keep track, you could try this once because it gives you a different kind of look at how you spend your money.

Just once, do the following things:

$ Make a list of what you spend your money on.

$ Write down the amount you spend, as best as you can, on each item.

$ List which are costs you can't change, like school lunch.

$ List those costs you can change, like a snack.

$ Take those that you can control and list them in order of the ones you like most.

Here's my list:

- $ Baseball card pack
- $ Crossword magazine
- $ Gum
- $ Slurpy
- $ Soda

By doing this, you know what you are spending and what you can eliminate because it is not important to you. Stop spending on the last thing or two on the list. Just cut them out altogether. You'll never miss them.

If you still don't have the money for the things you really want, go up the list and stop spending on all the things that are not important. If it's still not enough, shop around to get things cheaper.

And finally, if you still can't get all the stuff you want, you'll have to wait and save up for it. When you put away the money you used to spend on the stuff you didn't need or like, to get something better, this is called *savings* in Moneytalk.

Most kids save for things they can see, such as toys. Most grown-ups save for things they can't see, like "a rainy day" when they need the money for an emergency. But either way, the money is still yours so you can get what you want later.

Things I spend money on that I control:

1.
2.
3.
4.
5.
6.

Things from above list that I can't live without:
1.
2.
3.

Things that are great but I could do without:
1.
2.
3.

Things I spend on that I can cut out:
1.
2.
3.

5 Making the Most of Your Savings

Penelope Pennypincher and Steven Spender can work together to save money.

By now, you know that a budget helps you save money so that you can get what you really want in the future. It makes you richer and doesn't deprive you of anything. Since saving is so good, why do most people find it so hard to do?

Most people find it hard to save because they want everything right away. You *can* get just about all you want, but not immediately. Did you notice how your baby brother or sister cries when he or she doesn't get a bottle fast? Even big kids and grown-ups feel that way about getting things *now*! If you can feel better about waiting for what you want, you will save more and get better things later.

How to Make Saving Money Easier

Every time you get money, put some away immediately. Just put it in a drawer or piggy bank. I use an envelope hidden on a high shelf because my sister, who is two, keeps getting to it. She throws the money on the floor.

Shopping for Interest Rates

The younger you are when you start to save, the more money grows by the time you are twenty-one, for instance.

Take a look at how money grows if you start at our age: Here's how putting $1,000 in a bank will grow at given interest rates (added money given to you by the bank) until you are twenty-one.

Your starting age now with $1000 annual deposit:

% Interest	20	16	11	7	a new baby
		TOTAL EARNED BY AGE 21:			
5%	$1,050	$5,802	$13,207	$22,657	$34,719
8%	$1,080	$6,336	$15,645	$29,324	$49,423
11%	$1,110	$6,913	$18,561	$38,190	$71,265
14%	$1,140	$7,536	$22,045	$49,980	$103,768
17%	$1,170	$8,207	$26,200	$65,649	$152,139
20%	$1,200	$8,930	$31,150	$86,442	$224,026

As you see, interest is always a percentage. 5% means that you will get 5 extra pennies for every dollar you lent to the bank (put on deposit). Interest is credited—added to your account—every month, half-year, or year, depending on the bank or other borrower.

The best is every month. Why? Because if your interest also is earning interest (compounding), the faster the interest is added on, the more you will get back when the payback is made.

So start saving early. Also, you can see that the higher the interest rate, the better you will do. So you should shop around for a good rate. Here's how:

$ Ask the bank how often it credits your interest.

$ Get a chart of the rates they offer.

$ Find out if they pay less on small accounts.

$ Find out if they skip holidays in giving interest.

$ Find out whether, if you take out money before the end of the year, you still get interest up to the day you took it out. This is called *day-of-deposit to day-of-withdrawal crediting*.

$ Find out if the bank charges you any money if you don't keep putting money in all the time.

Part 2

THE KIDS' GUIDE TO MAKING MONEY WITH THEIR MONEY

Remember our juggler? One of the balls he tried to keep up in the air was called "making money grow."

You can get money through gifts, earnings, and other ways. You have just read about keeping your money by using goals, budgets, and savings. But a very hard job that you will eventually have is using your saved money to make even more money. Why do we need to do this?

There are two reasons it's important that you use your saved money to earn more money. The first is that one day you will stop working. This is called *retirement*. It's pretty hard to imagine retiring even before you have your first job. But as I understand it, it's a time when you have saved enough money that's making more money for you so that you don't have to work. You might work anyway, but you don't have to.

The second reason that money must make money is inflation. Remember, that's when things cost more to buy. Sometimes prices go up more than your earnings from a job. Your money needs to earn money so you can keep up with the cost of living.

A lot of grown-ups think that making money grow is

even harder than earning it in the first place or keeping it in the second place. There is a good explanation for this. Every time you try to have your money make money for you, you must take a risk. The risk is that you will lose it. When I play tennis against my garage, I always take a risk that I will lose the ball on the roof if I play too hard. But if I don't take the risk and play soft, I usually don't get the ball over my imaginary net. I still have the ball, but I also have a low score in the game.

It seems that money is like that. To make money, you must take a little risk; to make more, a bigger risk. But it is pretty hard to judge whether the risk is right and worthwhile. I'm glad I'm getting used to the idea now, before I have to put a lot of real money on the line.

6

The Risks and Rewards of Money-making

If you get money and budget to save it, you would then like to see it grow. Even without earning, finding, winning, borrowing, or getting money as a gift, you can end up with more.

You already get the drift that interest is added to your savings if you put them in a real bank instead of a piggy bank. When you use your money to make more money, it's called *investing*. The original amount you saved is called *capital*. The amount added to it by investing is called *growth*.

With the help of your parents, you can make money with your money. You don't need a lot to start with. Many investments can be made with just $25. If you make the right choice, you'll end up with much more. But it's important to know that sometimes when you invest capital, you can lose your money! So let's see how investments work.

There are only two kinds of investing. Both are ways that your money can make money, but they are very different.

One way that your money makes money is *lending it to others in return for interest* (extra money they pay you for the right to borrow your money). This is usually very safe and sure. You get a stated amount of money back on a specific date. For example, if you lend your brother $10.00, and he promises to give you back $11.00, you have just made a deal to be paid an extra dollar. That is what it cost him to borrow your money. Stated in a percentage, that's a 10% interest rate.

Another way that your money makes money is by *buying something today that may be worth more tomorrow and then selling it*. For example, if you buy a baseball card for $1 and resell it later for $1.50 that's called a profit. When you buy stocks you also hope that you will sell later on at a profit. By waiting until the value goes up, your money can make a lot more money this way than by lending. But you can also lose money or make less. It's a risk.

My mom says that the hardest thing for grown-ups to understand is that money is always risked, at least a little, when you use it to make more money. Some grown-ups take too much risk and some too little. But either way, it makes most of them uncomfortable. Adults take risks anyway, because the most money can be made from the riskiest investments. If they have extra money they can afford to lose, they may even take big chances, called *speculation*. There is a great game that teaches you all about risk taking for big profits. "$peculation: The Ultimate Trading Game," by Cayla Games, Inc., is for kids ages twelve and up. Of course, there can also be big losses in the game too.

The Totally Awesome Risk/Reward Game for Kids (and Their Parents)

Here's a fun way to see how different risks bring different rewards. You can play this game 100 times and never come out with exactly the same result. All you need is a single die.

Each player can start on any Start space. When it is your turn, roll the die and move the number of spaces it says. Follow the instructions on the space on which you landed. The first player to finish wins.

Who won when you played? Was it the player who started on Path 1, the most risky? He or she could be sent back to Start. Or was the winner the one who took Path 5, the longest path but the one with no risk. Or maybe the player who started on Path 2, 3, or 4, with a different mix of length and risk, won.

Start 1	Back To Start	Lose Turn				Go To End		Back To Start		
Start 2	Lose Turn	Lose Turn	Back To Start	Go To End		Lose Turn				
Start 3		Lose Turn	Move Ahead 2 Spaces	Lose Turn		Go Back 1 Space		Move Ahead 2 Spaces	Lose Turn	
Start 4			Go Back 1 Space		Lose Turn		Go Back 1 Space			Lose Turn
Start 5										

The more times you play, the more you will get different results. That's just like money. There are many roads to success and many combinations of risk (lose a turn) and reward (go to end). Which player would you like to be? The winner who takes the most risk? The winner who takes longer and has no risk? Or the one who takes a combination of risk and reward?

Some investments are absolutely safe, like lending your money to the U.S. government when you buy a savings bond. Others involve risks, like buying stocks. We will read about both. Different types of risk and reward combinations are right for different people and even for the same person at different times in his or her life.

Back To Start	**Lose Turn**			**Go To End**		**Back To Start**		**End 1**		
Lose Turn	**Lose Turn**	**Back To Start**		**Go To End**		**Lose Turn**		**End 2**		
	Lose Turn	**Move Ahead 2 Spaces**	**Lose Turn**		**Go Back 1 Space**		**Move Ahead 2 Spaces**	**Lose Turn**		**End 3**
		Go Back 1 Space		**Lose Turn**		**Go Back 1 Space**			**Lose Turn**	**End 4**
										End 5

7 Making Money by Lending Your Money to Others

One way to invest is to lend your money to others. They use your money for something they want and give you back more money than you gave them. They are paying you for the chance to use your money for a while.

This is exactly what happens when you put money in a bank savings account. When you open an account with $10 of your money, it will grow without you doing anything more. This happens because the bank gives you new money called *interest*. Why do they pay you for leaving money with them?

Here's the secret: Your $10 isn't really sitting in the account. The bank is using your money. It is investing it and making money for itself. That means the bank wants to use your money for as long as you let it. To get the use of your money, it will pay you. Lots of kids feel afraid or intimidated in a bank. It was built for grown-ups, and sometimes the building looks very big. But when you walk into a bank to put money in an account, even if it is one penny, you are the boss. You are lending your money to the bank, and the bank wants something you have. There are lots of banks, but there is only one you. That makes you very important.

It's much easier to win at moneymaking when your eyes are wide open.

The Bull's-Eye Game

Try this Bull's-Eye game. Take a coin. Close your eyes. Try to flip the coin into one of the circles with your eyes closed. Almost impossible! Now flip it with your eyes open. I bet you did better. Finally, keep your eyes open and place the coin in the center. You can't miss!

It's the same with investment decisions; keeping your eyes open is like having knowledge. Placing instead of flipping is like taking it easy, taking your time, and not getting pushed into a decision too fast.

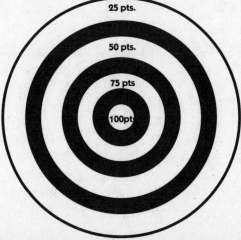

CDs

CD in Moneytalk stands for *certificate of deposit.* It's a way of lending money to a bank for a specific period of time, from a month to five years, in return for interest.

Things to Know Before You Lend Your Money

Before you lend your money to a bank or to anyone else, there are some things you should find out:

How safe is your money? When you lend your capital (money), you want it back someday. Money in banks is very safe because even if the bank goes out of business, the federal government will make sure you get your money back. This is called *FDIC insurance. FDIC* stands for *Federal Deposit Insurance Corporation.* It is an agency of the U.S. government set up in 1933 to pay you back your money if the bank can't.

How safe is the interest you are getting? After all, you are lending your money to the bank for a reason. The reason is to get interest added to your dollars. To be sure that you will really get what you expect, you want a promise that the interest will be paid. This promise is called a *guarantee*. The federal government also guarantees your interest with FDIC insurance. Everyone is insured up to $100,000, so I don't think we kids have to worry.

When will you get your money back? When you lend money, you can make different arrangements about when you get it back. In most cases, you can take your money back whenever you want it; this is called making a *with-*

drawal. The bank can't stop you. You get back all your capital plus any interest you earned on your money. But you can also arrange to let the bank keep your money until a certain date. You can't ask for it back before then, even if you need it. The date that you can get back the money is called the *maturity date*. Usually you will get a higher percentage of interest if you promise not to take back the money before a certain date.

How much money will your money make? What you are really asking in Moneytalk is, "How much interest will my capital earn?" That depends. Anyone who wants to borrow your money wants to pay you as little as possible. Don't get mad; that's just good business. The amount they pay in interest depends on some complicated economic things, such as how much they can make by using your money and how much other banks are willing to pay.

Money Riddles

Q. Why is Washington, D.C., like the money you put in the bank?

A. Because they are both called the "capital."

Q. Why do you never get bored when you put your money in a bank?

A. Because it keeps giving you interest.

Q. Why can't you see the money in the bank?

A. Because the bank invested it elsewhere.

Q. Why does your bond get serious when you cash it in?

A. Because it reached its maturity date.

8
Surprising Answers to the Question "Who Wants to Borrow a Kid's Money?"

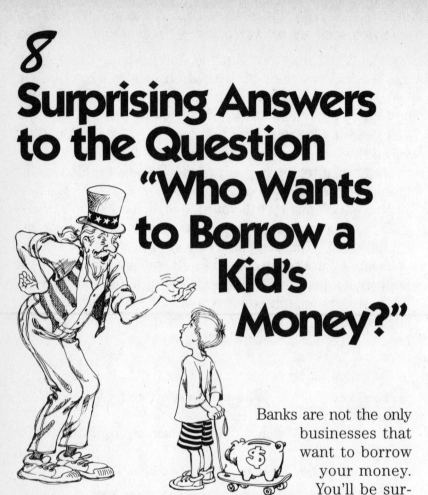

Banks are not the only businesses that want to borrow your money. You'll be surprised to find out how many ways there are to lend your money in return for interest. Sometimes it's hard to decide which one you want to do business with. This chapter tells you about some other ways to make money by lending your money.

The U.S. Government

The U.S. government wants to borrow your money in return for giving you interest. If you lend it your money, you get proof of the loan by getting a Series EE bond, also called a *U.S. Savings Bond*. You can buy one for $25. So a bond is only paper that shows that the government owes you money.

As usual, you will get interest back on your money and a date when you can get the capital and interest back. The amount of interest you get depends on how long you leave your money with the government. Here is the rule in action: The longer you agree to lend your money, the higher the interest. In Moneytalk, the day you get the money back is called the *maturity date*. You must leave the money in for at least six months.

These bonds are very safe, so of course interest rates are not as high as those on some other types of lending. As you know, the safer your money is when you lend it, the less interest the borrower must pay you to get you to lend money.

Things to Do
To get more information about U.S. government bonds, write to the Bureau of the Public Debt, Securities Transaction Branch, Washington, D.C. 20226, or call 1-800-US BONDS.

Cities and States

The *municipality* (city or town) and the state in which you live also want to borrow your money. They also will give you interest, a maturity date, and proof of the loan. This type of borrowing is called *municipal borrowing,* and the proof that you lent the money is called a *municipal bond.*

When you lend money to a municipality, you must be much more careful about its safety than you are with banks or the federal government, because even governments can have money trouble. If they do, they may not pay you back. In Moneytalk, this is called a *default*. Municipal bond defaults are very rare. Still, the possibility worries a lot of people.

To make investing in municipal bonds easier, two companies rate the bonds for safety. Just as you get a grade in school, cities and states get a grade for the safety of their bonds. One company is Standard & Poor's; it grades bonds from AAA to D. The other company is Moody's; it grades bonds from aaa to d.

Can you guess which pays more interest to you, a high-grade bond or a low-grade bond? That's right. A low-grade bond pays more interest because the city or state must give you an extra bonus to get you to take the chance on less safety.

Another thing that can happen with a municipal bond is that you may get paid back earlier (but never later) than the maturity date. This is a *call* in Moneytalk. You don't lose any of your money, but it can make you angry. You get angry for two reasons. First, interest is only paid up to the call date, but you were expecting to be paid up to the date of maturity. Second, now you must find a new place to lend your money, and interest rates may have gone down. In fact, that's probably why a bond is called in the first place. The municipality was able to pay you back fast and borrow new money from others at a lower rate.

Here's what happened to me: My mom lent money to a municipality in return for a high interest rate. The maturity date, the date we were going to get our money back, was the same year that I would turn eighteen. My mom wanted to use the money for college. Last year, the municipality called the bond. It paid us back our money with the interest earned seven years earlier than expected. Now my mom has to find a new bond, and interest rates are much lower than they were when she bought the old bond six years ago.

Oh, well, at least there is one good thing about municipal bonds: When you get interest, there is no tax to pay. The Constitution of the United States doesn't let the federal government tax money paid to you in return for lending your money to a city or state. In Chapter 21, you will read a lot about taxes, and you will see that this can be important.

Corporations

Big companies such as Nike, General Motors, Disney, and most that you can think of also want to borrow your money. They give you proof of the loan called a *corporate bond*. The same companies that grade municipal bonds (Standard & Poor's and Moody's) grade corporate bonds. Corporate bonds also have maturity dates and can be called (paid back) early. Some bonds can't be called because they have a *call protection* feature, a promise that they will last until maturity or at least until a specific date. I wish my bonds had that.

Lending Your Money

Lots of businesses and institutions and governments want to borrow your money. But with most of them you must invest at least $1,000, with some a lot more. So most of us aren't ready to make that kind of investment. For the future, just remember that no matter whom you lend your money to, the same rules apply. Always know:

$ How much interest you will get
$ When you will get your money back (what the maturity date is)
$ How safe your capital (money) is
$ How safe the interest that your money earns is

Einstein $E = MC^2$

Albert Einstein, one of the most brilliant men who ever lived, besides discovering the theory of relativity, also said, "Man's greatest invention is compound interest."

Why did Einstein say this? Because compound interest adds a lot to your savings.

Compound interest is added to your capital when the interest earned by the capital itself earns interest. The numbers are very impressive.

Let's say you start on February 1 with only a $0.01 saved. Let's say you double it every day. So you have $0.02 on February 2 and $0.04 by February 3. How long do you think it will take to have *$1 million*? Did you say 100 years, 10 years, 1 year? Starting with a penny and doubling every day, you would have over $1 million—$1,316,617.28, to be precise—in only 28 days! Awesome. This is how doubling per day would work:

AMOUNT	DATE	AMOUNT	DATE	AMOUNT	DATE
.01	2/1	10.24	2/11	10,485.76	2/21
.02	2/2	20.48	2/12	20,571.52	2/22
.04	2/3	40.96	2/13	41,143.04	2/23
.08	2/4	81.92	2/14	82,286.08	2/24
.16	2/5	163.84	2/15	164,572.16	2/25
.32	2/6	327.68	2/16	329,154.32	2/26
.64	2/7	655.36	2/17	658,308.64	2/27
1.28	2/8	1,310.72	2/18	1,316,617.28	2/28
2.56	2/9	2,621.44	2/19		
5.12	2/10	5,242.88	2/20		

No wonder Einstein was inspired. Of course, we know that your money won't double every day even with compound interest. But at 5 percent compound interest, you will see your $1,000 grow to $2,080 in 15 years; at 10 percent compound interest, the money will double in less than 8 years; and at 20 percent, it will double in only 3 years.

Here's what Einstein knew. He knew the *rule of 72*. Take the number 72 and divide it by the interest you are getting for lending your money. The result is the number of years it will take your money to double.

For example, if you are earning 9 percent interest, divide 72 by 9. The result, 8, is the number of years it will take to double your money. How many years will it take at 8 percent? Right. 9 years $(72 \div 8 = 9)$.

PENELOPE AND STEVEN SHOP FOR INTEREST

Steven got $25 from his grandfather as a birthday gift. Since he also got lots of toys from his friends, Steven was willing to put the money in the bank. Penelope also had $25. She saved it from the money her mother gave her to buy games and toys. Penelope and Steven both went shopping for the best interest rates they could get for lending their money to others.

They discovered that if they were willing to put money away for a long time and not use it, they would have quite a bit by the time they were ready for college. They also discovered that the interest rate would be 4 percent. They would get this by buying a $25 savings bond from the U.S.

government. To buy the bond, they would give the government $17.50 now. In ten years, earning 4 percent interest, the government would return to them $25.

Penelope and Steven both knew that they were really *lending* their money to the government in return for the interest they would earn. But the banker called it *buying a bond.*

The banker also told them that they could open up a bank account instead. If they did, they would get less interest—only 2 1/2 percent at the moment. This 2 1/2 percent interest would earn them $.63 per year for their $25 deposit. But each could get his or her money out any time it was wanted. There was no need to wait for a maturity date.

It was hard to decide whether to lend their money to the bank or to the government. Finally, Steven decided to lend his money to the U.S. government for a long time at a higher rate of interest. He did this because his goal was college, and saving for college was part of his plan. Penelope opted for the lower rate and the right to take her money at any time. After all, she thought, what if I need to buy something in a hurry and can't wait?

Would you choose not making much interest but being able to take your money out anytime? Or would you like to have a better chance of making more money but not getting it for a while? Why? How does your answer fit into your goals and plans?

9
Making Money:
Buying Things
Today That You
Can Sell
for More
Money
Tomorrow

Another way that your money can make money is to invest for *growth*. That means you buy something that becomes more valuable after a while. When it is worth more, you can sell it for more than you paid. In Moneytalk this is called *making a profit*. One example of a growth investment is stocks. *Stocks* are shares in a company. You can buy shares in lots of companies that you know, like PepsiCo or Coca-Cola. If you buy one share of stock in a company that has fifty shares, you actually own one-fiftieth of the company. In fact, most of the companies that want to borrow your money will sell you stock as well. You already know that if you lend money, you make money by getting interest in return for your loan. But if you invest for profit, there are no guarantees. You can make a lot more money than a lender, but you can also lose all or some of your *capital* (another word for money you invest).

How to Pick the Right Stocks to Make Money

When we talked about investing through lending, we worried about safety. And we solved our problem by looking at ratings and guarantees. Now, when we look at investing for profit, we worry about *risk*. Risk is Moneytalk for how likely you are to lose your money because what you buy (for example, a stock) goes down in value instead of up. We solve our problem by looking at how well the company is doing as a business. It's not hard for you to know which companies make a profit. Kids are some of the best stock pickers around. Just ask yourself and your friends these questions:

$ After school, what soda and snacks do you buy?
$ What video games do you like best?
$ What sneakers do you wear?
$ What clothing stores at the mall do you shop in?
$ What breakfast cereal do you eat?

When you hear of a company that a lot of kids like, you can do some research to find out if it is a moneymaker. Here's how:

$ Write to the company and ask for its annual report. This tells you how much the company earned last year. Compare the earnings to profits in prior years to see if the company is getting stronger.
$ Ask if the company has paid out a portion of the money it made to the stockholders. That is called paying a *dividend*. If so, you will receive money even before you sell at a profit.
$ Divide the last dividend paid by the company by the number of shares in the company. This is called

the *yield* in Moneytalk. Compare the yield with those of other stocks. If the yield is higher, the stock is doing well.

For Kids Who Really Love Stocks

If you really want to make stock picking a hobby, one way is to learn about buying stocks before they are popular with everyone else. Then sell them at a profit when the market is hot. Do this with a system called the *P/E,* which stands for *price/earnings ratio.* Every stock has one. The P/E tracks what other people will pay for a stock. *The trick is to buy a stock when the P/E is low, when no one wants it. Then sell when the P/E is high, when everyone will pay a high price.*

To find the P/E, divide last year's earnings per share into the price of the stock today. So if a stock costs $100 per share and earned $10 the P/E is 10 (100 divided by 10 is 10). A price/earnings ratio of 10 means that investors were willing to pay 10 times earnings for the stock. If the P/E is high, lots of investors want it, and it will cost a lot to buy. If the P/E is low, fewer investors are interested and it goes for a lower price.

A good rule of thumb is to use 12 as an average P/E. Today most stocks are expensive, some as high as 30. When this happens, it is thought that the market prices will eventually drop to lower the P/E, so many people wait before they buy stocks.

A market of high P/E stocks means people think the stocks will be worth even more later. This is called a *bull market.* When P/Es are low, people think stocks will go down. This is called a *bear market.*

So for kids who love to make money with stocks, and I am one of them, try this: Without really investing anything, pick and follow stocks in your local paper or in the *Wall Street Journal*. Lots of colleges already give pretend accounts to kids who participate in investing contests. A few lower schools are starting to do the same. But even if there is no organized contest at your school, you can have one right at home. You can do it yourself or compare the results with your parents, brothers and sisters, or friends. It's cool to see who made more money after three months, but you learn a lot if you check out the same stocks after six months and a year. If you do that, you really see how prices and your money go up and down. You also see that it's just as important to know when to sell as it is to choose a winning stock in the first place. In order to play this stock-picking game, you will have to know how to read the financial pages. You can also find the P/E fast from those pages once you know how to read them.

How to Read the Financial Pages

When you own a stock, you must find out how it is doing. You can do this by reading the financial pages in a newspaper such as the *Wall Street Journal* every day. This is not an easy thing to do at first. But once you get the hang of it, it will become easier. Before you go on, you must know that prices are measured in fractions of a dollar. These fractions are given in eighths, fourths, and halves. In dollars and cents they are:

fraction	dollars	cents
1/8	$0.125	12.5
1/4	$0.25	25
3/8	$0.375	37.5
1/2	$0.50	50
5/8	$0.625	62.5
3/4	$0.75	75
7/8	$0.875	87.5
1	$1.00	100

So $107⅝ would equal $107.625 per share.

Here is what a stock report looks like in the paper:

	1	2	3	4	5	6	7	8	9	10	11
	52-Week				Yld	P/E	Sales				
	High	Low	Stock - Div		%	Ratio	100s	High	Low	Last	Chg.
	15⅞	14¼	IntcpIMn.90	6.1			251	14⅞	14¾	14⅞	+ ⅛
	18½	15⅜	Intcapln 1.11a	6.5			128	17	16⅞	17	+ ⅛
	16¾	14	IntlMT 1.02a	6.2			376	16⅜	16⅛	16⅜	+ ¼
			IntNYQn				10	15	15	15	....
	15¾	14¼	IQMInc.99	6.3			805	15¾	15⅝	15¾	.....
	16⅝	14½	IQMInv 1.08a	6.7			306	16¼	16	16⅛	....
			IntQIMun				90	15	15	15	....
	15¾	6¾	Interco				56	14½	14¼	14⅜	— ⅛
	4¾	3⅛	Intrlke				96	3¾	3¾	3¾	....
	24½	19⅛	IntAlu 1.00		4.5	26	33	22¼	22⅛	22⅛	— ¼
	84⅝	40⅝	IBM 1.00		2.4		17091	42½	41⅝	41⅞	— ¼
	25⅞	24½	IBM pf 1.88	7.4			764	25¼	25	25¼	+ ⅛
	20⅝	9⅛	IntFam			24	276	21	20⅜	21	+ ⅞
	119½	103	IntFlav 3.00		2.8	22	x1938	114½	108⅛	108⅛	—4¾
	39¾	17⅞	IGame s.06i		.2	45	7287	39½	37½	39½	+2

Look at the numbers across from the arrow on the top of the chart. They are the numbers of the paragraphs that explain each column. Here they are:

1. *High for the Year:* The first column shows you the highest price per share your stock has been in the last 52 weeks.

2. *Low for the Year:* The second column shows you the lowest price per share your stock has been in the past 52 weeks.

3. *Stock:* The third column tells you which stock this chart refers to, in this case IBM.

4. *Dividends:* A *dividend* is a share of a company's profit that stockholders get. The figure in the paper shows the dividend per share for the current year. Some companies don't pay dividends at all. Some companies may have a dividend one year and not another.

5. % Yield: The *yield* is a measure of how well your stock is doing. Divide the dividend by the closing price to get the yield. Note: You want a high yield.

6. P/E Ratio (Price/Earnings Ratio): This shows how much other investors are willing to pay for a stock. It tells you whether the stock is a bargain or is overvalued. *P* stands for *price; E* stands for *earnings*. By dividing the earnings into the price, we find out how many times the earnings of a company other investors are willing to pay per share. If they will pay many times earnings, the stock may be too risky because if they change their mind, you won't be able to sell it for much more than you paid or will even have to sell for less.

7. Sales: This is the number of shares of the company's stock bought and sold *(traded)* in a day in hundredths. So 17091 would be 1,709,100 shares.

8. High: How high the price of the stock went that day.

9. Low: How low the price of the stock went that day.

10. Last: The last price of the stock that day *(closing price)*.

11. Change: This shows if your stock went up that day compared to what the last price was at the close on the day before. A plus sign means it went up, a minus sign means it went down. In this case, $-\frac{1}{4}$ or $.25 was the difference.

Investing in Barbie

The recent price of a share in Mattel, the company that makes Barbie, was recently $33. The 1993 P/E of 25 shows that lots of people are willing to pay a good price for Barbie's (Mattel's) stock.

Arthur's Stock Tips

$ Think of the companies you like and ask your friends.

$ Get the annual report and decide if the company is doing well by looking at the things you find in the report's appendix.

$ Check the P/E in the financial pages.

$ If the P/E is low (under 10 or 11), it looks like a winner.

Things to Do

Join a club. Write to the National Association of Investment Clubs, 1515 East Eleven Mile Road, Royal Oak, MI 48062, or call 313-543-0612. You will get information on forming a stock club or joining one in your area.

10

Stocks: How to Invest Money You Save from Your Allowance

"Guess who owns Nike, Disney, Pepsi, Coca-Cola, Reebok, and Nintendo. Me!"
—Paula

Some people think that you need to have a lot of money to invest in stock, even be a millionaire. That's not true. There are two ways that you can be an investor with as little as $10 (although $25 is even better).

Don't *"Be"* a DRIP: Buy One!

There is a program that most large companies have with the funny name of *DRIP*. It stands for *dividend reinvestment plan*. A *dividend* is the portion of the profits of a company that is paid out to the shareholders. When we discussed picking a good stock, one thing we looked for was whether the company pays out its profits as a dividend.

If it does, this dividend can be used to buy more shares in the company itself. This is called *reinvesting*. First, buy a share in a company. Then tell the company to take your dividends and buy more of its stock for you. You have started a DRIP.

Constant reinvesting buys more of a fraction of a share of stock. This goes on and on. Before you know it, you have quite a few dollars invested in the stock.

Unlike investments where you lend money, investing in stocks for profit has no maturity date. If you ever want to sell your shares, just call the DRIP's number and tell them to sell and send you the money. Try to watch the newspaper and sell when the value of the shares go up from the price you paid. That's how you make the biggest profit. *Buy low and sell high!*

Things to Do

To find out which companies have DRIPs and which will put you in the plan with only a few shares, write to Dow Theory Forecasts, Inc., 7412 Calumet Avenue, Hammond, IN 43624-2692, or call 219-931-6480.

Buying One Share

There are many ways that you can buy one or a few shares with your allowance so you can be part of a DRIP.

$ Join an NAIC stock club (see Chapter 9). Lots of companies you know, such as McDonald's, Disney, Kellogg, and Quaker Oats, let you buy one share if you belong to a club.

$ Write to the company of your choice. Some will sell one share directly. *Even if a share costs more money than you have, they will sell you a fraction of a share.*

Let's say that a share of Disney stock costs $75 and you have saved up $15 after making a budget. Just write to the company and ask them to buy as large a fraction of a share of Disney as $15 will buy.

$ Ask a *broker* if he or she can sell you a few shares. Most can. (We'll talk about brokers in Chapter 15.)

Remember, shares go up and down in value every day. So if you can buy when the share costs less, you will get more for your $15. This, in Moneytalk, is called *playing the market*. It takes time, reading, and experience.

Maybe someday you will be able to do this. For now, just call when you have the capital (money) to invest.

Matching Game: Stock Stuff

Match the definition to the word.

1. Undervalued stock

    A. Stock of companies that own real estate and equipment equal to or more than the value of their shares

2. Broker

    B. Stocks that don't trade on the stock exchange

3. Price/earnings ratio

    C. A person licensed to sell stocks, bonds, and other securities

4. Dividends

    D. The amount of profit a company pays out to its stockholders

5. Share

    E. An investor who thinks the price of stocks will go up

STOCKS 61

6. OTC stocks

F. Buying stocks with money you borrow from your broker. The stocks you own are "*collateral*."

7. Bull

G. An investor who thinks stocks will go down.

8. Bear

H. Shows whether investors are willing to pay a lot or a little for the stock

9. Buying on margin

I. Same as stock

Answers: 1 (A), 2 (C), 3 (H), 4 (D), 5 (I), 6 (B), 7 (E), 8 (G), 9 (F).

11

Totally Awesome: Stock Investment Plan for Kids Using Mutual Funds

"There are 4,000 mutual funds to choose from. Heavy."

—Paul

Another way to invest in stocks with very little money is to buy a share, not in a company, but in a mutual fund. A *mutual fund* is a pool of a lot of people's money that is used to buy a lot of shares of stocks in many different companies. The mutual fund manager makes all the decisions. The manager picks the companies she or he thinks will make a profit, decides when to sell, and even tries to judge which stocks will go up and down in value. Knowing who the manager is can be very important in picking a fund that does well.

In Moneytalk, a share in a mutual fund is called a *unit*. A few mutual funds will sell you a unit for $10, some insist on $25, and others ask for more. But since there are about 4,000 mutual funds in this country, you'll find one in which to invest.

Before you buy, you'll get a booklet called a *prospectus*. Even though you may fall asleep a few times trying to read the important parts, it's worth it. It tells you things like:

$ What a fund invests in
$ Who the manager is
$ The expenses you pay
$ The goals of the fund

The "All the Eggs in One Basket" Game

You have 10 eggs that you have just taken from the chicken house. The Fox wants the eggs but can only carry 1 basket. You have 10 baskets. Each basket holds from 1 to 10 eggs. What is the best way to put the eggs in the baskets to make them safe from the Fox?

Well, it's your choice. If you put all the eggs in one basket, you will keep all the eggs 9 out of 10 times. But if the Fox gets a hold of that basket, you lose everything. If you put 1 egg in each basket, you may lose one to the Fox while you handle all the others. But at least the other 9 are safe.

This way of protecting what you have is called "diversification." If you put all your eggs in one basket, you may lose everything one day. If you put one egg in each, you'll probably lose at least one but not more. A good idea is to handle three or four baskets—not too many to keep track of, but still enough to give you a lot of eggs left if the Fox steals one.

Mutual funds help you put your (nest) egg in a lot of baskets. They make it easy to diversify. The great thing about a mutual fund is that you get a tiny part of lots of different stocks. This way, you don't have to choose only one company that you like. It gives you many different investments. So if one company isn't doing very well, another might be. This cuts your risk. Because kids don't usually have a lot of money to invest, there is really no other way for us to diversify except in mutual funds.

Dollar Cost Averaging:
How Any Kid Can Be a Great Investor

There is a special system for people with small amounts of money to invest that gives you the most profit. It can make any kid a great investor, and it's easy to follow. In Moneytalk, it's called *dollar cost averaging*, or *DCA*. It works best with mutual funds.

All you need is a little extra money for investing every week. A dollar is good enough; more is OK, too.

Next, decide what you want to invest in. You can pick a single stock in a DRIP or a mutual fund. DCA doesn't work with the type of investing that is really lending.

After you pick your mutual fund or DRIP, buy more every week or month. *The trick is to put exactly the same amount into the investment each time.* If you do, a funny thing happens. You end up buying more of the stocks or units at a lower price than at a higher price. As you know, the best way to make a profit is to buy low and sell high. With dollar cost averaging, you buy low, so you are halfway there.

To understand why, you have to do some math and understand how averages work. With or without the math, the idea is easy. Just save the same amount of money each week, and use it to make an investment in the same stock or mutual fund. By the time you go to sell, you will have paid less for each share or unit than if you had lots of money and bought all at once.

Things to Do

For a list of mutual funds that charge no commissions (no-load funds), write to:

One Hundred Percent No-Load Mutual Fund Council, 1501 Broadway, Suite 312, New York, NY 10036, or call 212-768-2477

Mutual Fund Education Alliance, 1900 Erie Street, Suite 120, Kansas City, MO 64116, or call 816-471-1454

PAULA BUYS A MONEY TREE

Paula is eleven years old. She told her parents that she saw a show about how important college is. She wanted to start saving for it. Her parents gave her $50 to start her college fund. But Paula didn't know how to begin, so she asked her parents' broker what to do. The broker told her she could choose from stocks, bonds, and mutual funds. She looked at stocks but thought that they were too risky. She didn't like bonds because they didn't make as much money as she wanted.

Then she looked at mutual funds. She saw that they are a group of stocks and that they are a little safer. She looked further into kinds of mutual funds: *growth, income,* and some others. She looked at all of them. She saw that a *growth mutual fund* was for people who could wait for their money for several years. She also saw that *income mutual funds* were best for people who needed money now. She thought that a growth mutual fund would be better for her college fund.

What things would you like to think about before *you* make an investment decision?

Here's my list:

1. What is my goal or purpose? (for example, growth for the future, or buying something I need but don't have the money for getting)

2. Can I afford to make this investment? What's the minimum I need to invest? (for example, $250 for a mutual fund, or $1.50 for a baseball card)

3. In the past, how much money has been made by investments like the one I'm thinking about? During what time period?

4. Can I sell and get my money back anytime I want, or do I have to wait for a maturity date?

5. Are there any guarantees or can I lose all or part of my money?

6. Who controls or manages the investment? (for example, is it a mutual fund manager?)

7. Do I already have too many investments like this one?

8. What are the fees or costs to make the investment?

12
Other Stuff You Can Buy to Make a Profit

"Do I want real estate or collectibles? Hmm, I think I'll collect real estate!"
—Marvin Mogul

You can invest capital for profit in lots of things. Almost anything that can be sold can make you money. *Just remember to buy low and sell high.* But this is easier said than done.

Most things that make a profit are too expensive for kids to invest in. So when I thought about them—things like real estate, gold, and oil that grown-ups talk about to make money—I said, "No way!" But then I found out that all these things can also be bought with a unit in a mutual fund. So I said, "Way!" When we get older and have more money, we can buy them with or without a fund. Here are some amazing things that can be invested in through a mutual fund.

Real Estate

Real estate is Moneytalk for *property* such as a house and land or a bunch of stores or malls. A mutual fund called a *REIT,* or *real estate investment trust,* owns property (real estate) and manages it for all the investors. The property is owned by everyone through a trust. A *trust* is a made-up legal thing where one person manages something for the benefit of others. Just as a stock mutual fund owns a lot of stocks, a REIT owns a lot of property.

Commodities

That's Moneytalk for stuff. A *commodity* can be anything that is bought and sold all the time. Some examples are gold, silver, metals, farm products such as meat and soybeans, and even foreign currency. These investments have the most risk because they have no guarantees like lending does and they have no reliable past-performance records like the stock companies do. But many people invest in them because they believe the risk is worth the chance to make lots of money.

Collectibles

Here's one investment that doesn't need a mutual fund. I have a baseball card collection. Do you collect anything? If you do, you are already an investor. A *collectible* is anything that you buy and can resell at a profit. Sound familiar? If you do collect stuff that you can resell, answer these questions about your collection. They will tell you a lot about the type of investor you are.

$ Do you collect lots of inexpensive things, like postage stamps that are not rare yet, or a few big, expensive things, like dolls?

$ Do you pay attention to the cost and resale value?
$ Do you keep a record of the cost?
$ Have you ever thought of selling some of the things in your collection for a profit?
$ Do you trade with your friends?
$ Do you know any dealers in your area personally?

To have a successful collection, you must do many things.

1. You must be serious.
2. You must keep good records. For example:
   $ When you buy something for your collection, always keep a receipt.
   $ Put the receipts in a folder for safekeeping.
   $ When you sell, keep a record of the price you got.
3. Keep an inventory of what you have, its cost and what it's worth today. You can look up the value of collectibles in *Kovels' Know Your Collectibles Price List*, Crown, 1993.
4. Always keep your collection in *mint condition* (the best). It gets the most money on resale.

KOLLECTING KATIE AND THE BASEBALL CARD SALE

Katie was ten, and a real fan of baseball cards. In fact, her room was cluttered with them. She didn't know how to get rid of them because she didn't want to give them away or throw them away. So she asked her brother, Tom, what to do. He said, "Sell them at a profit, sort of like a garage sale."

"Great idea," said Katie. She gathered most of her cards (she kept some so that she wouldn't have to restart her collection from ground zero). She also bought a magazine that told her the prices of all the baseball cards. She held the sale on Saturday and sold all of her cards at a profit.

COLLECTOR'S RECORD

Item Bought	Price Paid	Today's Value (Update Every Six Months)	Date Sold	Price Received

Do you think that having the sale was the right decision?

MARVIN MOGUL AND THE REAL ESTATE DEAL

Marvin Mogul is twelve years old and would like to be a real estate agent. That means he will make money helping other people buy and sell their property. He will be paid a percentage of the sale price of the property, usually by the seller. But he only makes money if the sale goes through.

To practice for his future, Marvin decided to help kids sell playhouses they build. (Marvin is making an extra profit by selling the plans for these houses.) But he is having trouble selling one of the houses. It costs $40, and nobody wants to buy it. He doesn't know what to do.

He asked his friends what to do. None of them knew. Then, after two weeks, Marvin got an idea: Maybe he should lower the price. He did, and he sold the house in a week.

What are some things you would do to make a playhouse or anything else sell faster?

Discuss your ideas with your parents.

13
How to Save the Planet

"Investing right can help make a better world."
—Responsible Rhoda

The best part of investing is that it gives you a say in lots of things. In school and at home, I learn about stuff that's very wrong with the world. Sometimes, it scares me. Things like the ozone layer, oil spills, and governments that deny human rights also make me angry. But, hey, I'm just a kid, so what can I do about it?

Once I become an investor, I can do plenty. Any stock owner, even one with only one share, can go to a stockholders' meeting. Most of the time, the meetings are held once a year. At the meeting, anyone can speak up about the company. If it pollutes the environment or does anything else you don't like, you can say so. If you can't get to the meeting, you can write.

But more powerful than speaking up at meetings is choosing to invest in companies that don't do the things you are against and that try to do the things you are for.

There are companies that make a special effort to clean up the environment, don't do business with countries that deny civil rights, and treat women and minorities fairly.

In Moneytalk, investing in these companies is called *socially responsible investing*. Too bad all companies aren't socially responsible. Maybe we can make them that way when we grow up and become businesspeople.

Today, some areas of socially responsible investing are companies that work on forestation, water resources, safer and cheaper energy, better waste disposal, and control of noise and other kinds of pollution. Asian and European companies are growing fastest in these areas.

Things to Do

If you like the idea of making money in a socially responsible way, you can do it with our old friend the mutual fund. Here are the names of a few:

$ **Global Environment Fund, 1250 24th Street, NW, Suite 300, Washington, DC 20037**
$ **Domini Social Index Trust, 1-800-762-8814**
$ **Calvert Social Investment Fund, 1-800-368-2748**
$ **Righttime Social Awareness Fund, 1-800-242-1421**
$ **Pax World Fund, 1-800-767-1729**

For a list of lots more, write to Social Investment Forum, 430 First Avenue N, Suite 290, Minneapolis, MN 55401, or call 612-333-8338.

It's important to know that just because a company is socially responsible doesn't mean you make more money. Sometimes, the most money is made by companies that do things you don't like. One of the toughest decisions for an investor to make is whether to try to make money or to make a little less with a socially responsible attitude.

This is what I do when I read the boring prospectus: If

the fund does well and also does good things for the environment, that's my choice. If a fund or company makes a lot of money and I read in the papers that it did a bad thing, I just don't invest, even if I could make a profit. If a company is neutral, I'll invest in that, too. Every kid must make his or her own decisions. How do you feel about it?

GERALD INVESTS IN HIS FUTURE

Gerald was ten years old, and had just received $25 from his parents as a Christmas gift. He decided to invest it. But he didn't know how to do this, so he went to the magazine store and bought a copy of the *Wall Street Journal*.

Around this same time, he saw a TV show about the environment. He wanted to save it. He wanted to invest in companies that he believed were doing the right thing about the environment. He also wanted companies that were hiring men and women equally. He found a new company that was researching cheaper ways to recycle paper. It was $1 a share, so Gerald bought 25 shares.

What do you want your perfect company to be like?

14
Where in the World Is Your Money?

Kids can have their money make money from investments in many parts of the world. With the awesome technology we have, by the time we are older, all of us will be invested in almost every country and have stocks in foreign companies. Imagine yourself lending money to France or Korea!

In Moneytalk, this is called *global investing*. You can start right now to be a global investor. Here's how.

International Mutual Funds

Remember the mutual fund? You buy a unit in the mutual fund, and that gives you a small share in the hundreds of investments owned by the fund. The cool thing is that these foreign investments can be in almost anything that makes a profit: stocks, real estate, gold, even money lent to foreign governments. If you buy a global or international mutual fund, you own a piece of lots of foreign companies.

There are even funds that concentrate on one country at a time, like the Spain and the Philippine Funds. Right now some countries, like Mexico and Brazil, are "hot." They are called *emerging growth countries*, in Moneytalk. Some people believe that they will become big-profit countries. It's hard to tell, so these are risky. Other countries, like most of those in Europe, have been doing business for a long time and are safer, but may not give you as much profit. Even in global investing, you always have to balance the risk and the reward.

Other Ways to Make a Profit in Foreign Countries

Mutual funds are not the only way to invest in foreign stocks. Many foreign companies sell stock through U.S. *brokers*, professionals who are licensed to sell stock. You'll find out how to buy stock from them in Chapter 15.

Some companies don't sell stock through U.S. brokers or mutual funds. But you can invest in them by buying *ADRs*, or *American Depository Receipts*. These are proof that you bought a foreign stock, and the proof is held in a bank outside the United States. As kids, we probably will never buy an ADR. But it's good to know they exist because when we grow up we will be more likely to invest in foreign companies than our parents and grandparents. The world is growing smaller, and investment choices are available in every country. This is called the *global economy*. By the time we are grown-ups we will have less resistance to investing around the world. Also, we might win the lottery, travel abroad, and get interested in a foreign company. Hey, you never know!

Lending Money to the King

Another way to make money globally is to lend money to foreign governments and companies. This is just like buying U.S. government and corporate bonds, which you read about in Chapter 8. All the same rules apply.

$ You know the safety of capital and interest.
$ You know when you can get your money back.
$ You know the interest you will get.

And guess what? There are mutual funds that own only foreign corporate and government bonds. They are called *foreign income funds*. Some of the countries in these funds are run by kings and queens. So it's like lending your money to royalty.

There is even a bank in Missouri called the Mark Twain Bank, after the author of *The Adventures of Huckleberry Finn*, that will open a bank account in any of twelve different types of foreign money. They take a minimum of $10,000, which is a fortune for a kid. But my mom says that one day soon every bank will have accounts in foreign money, even for small investors like us.

Currency: The Most Super Fun to Have with Money

Maybe you are wondering how buying foreign money makes money. I learned about it on a trip I took to England. I noticed that my mom had U.S. dollars but that all the prices were in English pounds (that's what paper money is called in England).

Since the stores, hotels, and restaurants didn't accept dollars, we had to change them (*convert*, in Moneytalk) into pounds. The tricky part was that one dollar did not equal one pound. And what was more confusing, the amount of dollars a pound did equal changed every day. One day a pound cost $1.40; another day it cost $1.45. Of course, the fewer dollars my mother paid for the pounds, the happier she was. This was getting interesting.

At the end of the trip, my mother had lots of pounds left. Now she had to convert the pounds back into dollars. On the day we left for home, the pound equaled $1.43. That meant that my mom made 3 cents for every pound she converted that she bought at $1.40 and lost 2 cents on every pound that she bought at $1.45.

That's how I learned that you can make and lose money

on *currency conversion,* or *exchange.* It's another way to invest. It's risky, but it sure is a lot of fun.

The main thing to remember is that every time you make any kind of global investment, you are also investing in the currency involved in the investment.

This is especially true if you are lending your money to a foreign government or company and getting a bond back. At the maturity date, you will get your money back in foreign currency. When you convert it to dollars, you may make or lose money on the exchange. So, like Doublemint gum, a foreign investment is "Two, two, two investments in one!"—an investment in stocks or bonds and in the currency of the country.

The World of Money Game

Unscramble the unit of currency in column A and then match it with the country in column B.

Column A	Column B
1. darn	a. India
2. ad roll	b. Italy
3. pose	c. Russia
4. rail	d. Canada
5. nest girl	e. Mexico
6. pure e	f. Spain
7. luber	g. England
8. pat see	h. South Africa

Answers: 1. rand (h) 2. dollar (d) 3. peso (e) 4. lira (b) 5. sterling (g) 6. rupee (a) 7. ruble (c) 8. peseta (f)

15
Bankers, Brokers, Financial Planners, & Other Money Experts

There are many types of professionals who can help you handle your money. They all do different things, have different titles, work in different kinds of places, and had different educations. I spoke to a lot of them while writing this book. I can tell you one thing: They all like to talk to kids. Don't ever be afraid to ask them questions. That's a big part of their jobs. Here is who they are and what they can do for you.

Bankers

Banker is a word for many kinds of people who work in a bank. The one you'll probably meet first is the *teller*. That person takes your money and puts it into your savings or checking account.

Another type of banker is a *loan officer*. He or she sees

if the bank is willing to lend you money. (You'll read all about loan officers in Chapter 16.)

A third type of banker is the *bank manager*. This person makes sure the bank is running smoothly and handles your complaints.

Finally, there is the *president* of the bank and the people on the *board of directors*. As you know, banks borrow your money and use it to invest for profit. These bankers, among other things, decide how the bank's money will be invested.

Brokers

Brokers are people who have taken and passed a special exam that allows them to buy and sell stocks and bonds. Without this license, they can't make trades for you. Brokers study different types of investments and also make suggestions about what you should buy. You can make your own choices or follow your broker's advice. Most investors do a little bit of both.

Stocks are traded through *stock exchanges* that are under heavy government regulation. It's very important that people like us who buy and sell stock do so in a fair market. So the stock salesmen or brokers must be licensed.

Things to Do
Write for a free book, by postcard, that tells you how the stock market works: "Journey Through a Stock Exchange," American Stock Exchange Publication Services, 86 Trinity Place, New York, NY 10006.

Brokers get paid every time you buy or sell a stock or bond. Sometimes they get a percentage of the purchase or sale price. This is called a *commission*, in Moneytalk. It is usually used with stocks.

Sometimes brokers get a *markup* instead of a commission. A markup is Moneytalk for the difference between what they pay for the item and the price at which they buy it for you. A markup is usually the way the broker gets paid for buying bonds for you.

Guess who pays the broker the commission or markup. You!

That's why many people like to use special brokers called *discount brokers*. They charge a set price, depending on the size of your investment, that is lower than what most other brokers charge. But many times they don't give you advice; they just make trades.

To us kids, the commission a broker gets is very important because we have so little to invest that the broker's fee can be more than our investment. For example, $37 is the minimum charge in some companies.

Also, brokers' fees are lowest if an investor buys at least 100 shares of a stock. This is called a *round lot,* in Moneytalk. Most kids can only buy a couple of shares. A sale of less than 100 is called an *odd lot.* So even though we didn't buy much, we end up paying more in commission.

That's why I like DRIPs, which are discussed in Chapter 10. There is no commission at all. Also, some mutual funds can be bought without a commission. They are called *no-load funds,* in Moneytalk. Still, it's better to have a good investment that costs a commission than a bad one that is commission-free. But how do you know which investment is right for you?

Financial Planners: New Kids on the Block

Financial planners are newcomers on the money front. They are people who help you decide which investments are best for you. They look at your income, expenses, and how much risk you want to take. They also look at your goals and when you want to achieve them. With all this information, they make a special plan for you to follow.

Financial planners are not licensed. But a lot of them are *CFPs, Certified Financial Planners*. To be certified, they must take special courses and pass examinations.

Sometimes financial planners are also brokers. If so, they also get a markup or commission if you buy what they suggest. Sometimes they are paid for their time by the hour. The average financial plan takes about twenty hours to do and is hard work. It can get expensive. Because of this, most planners make money through commissions.

Real Estate Agents

A *real estate agent* or *broker* helps you find and buy property. This includes a house, land, and stores you want to rent or buy. They get a commission, usually around 6 percent of the sale price or two months' rent.

Insurance Salesmen

Insurance salesmen sell you life, health, auto, and home insurance. It is a way of reducing your money worries if you have a disaster.

Lawyers, Accountants, and CPAs

There are many other professionals who may help you with your money. *Lawyers* and *accountants* can help prepare taxes, give business advice, and negotiate deals for you.

Some accountants take a special exam that certifies them. They are called *CPAs,* or *certified public accountants.* They can help you with your taxes and also act for you in front of the government agency that collects taxes. That agency is called the *IRS,* or *Internal Revenue Service.* You'll read about it in Chapter 21.

Match the Professionals Game

Match the professionals with the things they do for you.

1. Buying life insurance	**a. Financial planner**
2. Making a financial portfolio	**b. Banker**
3. Granting a loan	**c. Real estate agent**
4. Selling a house	**d. Insurance salesman**
5. Buying auto insurance	**e. Stockbroker**
6. Buying stock	**f. Lawyer**
7. Doing your taxes	**g. Insurance salesman**
8. Closing on property	**h. Accountant**

Answers: a (2), b (3), c (4), d (1), e (6), f (8), g (5), h (7)

Read This Before You Buy from a Broker

$ A *regular broker* charges you a percentage of the price of the stocks and bonds you buy or sell. So if you buy $2,000 worth of stock, it might cost you $70.

$ A *discount broker* charges you a smaller percentage of the price. So, a $2,000 buy could cost only $40.

$ A *deep-discount broker* charges, not by the price, but by the number of shares. This can be much cheaper if you make a big purchase or sale. But they usually charge a minimum of $37, so we small investors don't save much.

$ *DRIPs* avoid brokers altogether, because you buy directly from the company at no cost. This is a great idea for kids, but not all companies do it.

Here's what I do about brokers:

I have one regular broker to give advice, research, and direction, even though it costs a little more. And I have one discount broker when I know just what I want and don't need to talk to anyone. I buy through DRIPs whenever I can.

Part 3

CREDIT & DEBT: TWO SIDES OF THE SAME COIN

"*Don't take one if you don't want the other.*"
—Candy Creditworthy

Sometimes you can't save enough money to get what you want. When that happens, there may be someone who is willing to let you use his or her money as long as you pay them back with interest. If you read Chapter 8 on investing, you already know that banks, corporations, and governments offer you interest in order to use your money. Well, you must do the same in order to borrow money from them or from anyone else.

In Moneytalk, when you use someone else's money to get something you want, it's called *borrowing*. As a borrower, you must pay back the money with extra money called *interest*. If you are the one letting others use your money, it's called *lending*. You are the lender, and you get your money back someday with interest.

In Moneytalk, the ability to borrow money is called *credit*. Everyone wants credit in case they need to buy something they can't afford right away. But here's the catch: Once you use the credit, you must pay back the money. This responsibility to pay back is called *debt*. No one likes to be in debt, even though most Americans are.

The Marble-Borrowing Game

In order to play in a marbles tournament, you need 100 marbles. Pretend you have only 50 and need 50 more. What can you do? You can promise to pay 10 marbles a day for 6 days to someone if he or she lets you borrow the marbles. This will pay back the player who lends you the marbles 60 all told—50 for what was lent plus 10 as interest. But you'd better win the tournament, or you won't have any marbles to pay back.

I guess this isn't much of a game. But by the time you owe so much, you've probably lost your marbles!

16
How Expensive Is Money to Borrow?

All the things you wanted to know when you invest by lending (see Chapter 7) are the things a lender wants to know when you borrow money from him or her. How sure are they that you will pay them back? A person who has borrowed money before and has a good record of paying back is a good choice for a lender. Willingness of a lender to trust you is called your *creditworthiness*, in Moneytalk. The amount they are willing to lend to you is called your *line of credit*. If you have a record of failure to pay, your creditworthiness is low and you may not be able to get a line of credit. In that case, to borrow money you must pay a lot more interest to get the lender to take the risk that you'll pay this time. Also, the lender will ask:

$ How long do you want to keep the money?
Most of the time, the longer you want to keep the

money the lower the interest rate. Short-term borrowing is more expensive. This always sounds funny to me. But there is a reason. A lender has to work hard to check out your creditworthiness. Once they are satisfied that they can trust you, they want you to keep their money and pay them interest every year. If you pay them off fast, they have to find someone else to lend to. That's extra work. So lenders will charge a creditworthy person less interest if he or she sticks with the loan for a long time.

$ How much do you want to borrow?
Maybe you can guess that usually the more you borrow, the lower the interest is. That's for the same reason we just saw. The lender only has to work hard once to find a borrower who wants to borrow a lot of money. It's easier than finding loads of small borrowers.

So it actually costs less to borrow a lot than a little. Unfortunately, most people don't get the interest rate break. Borrowers like corporations borrow so much that they get a discount on the interest rate. This is called *prime rate,* in Moneytalk. It's a cheaper way of borrowing than individuals ever get. Bummer! Still, the rates we are charged for borrowing are usually based on a few percentage points more than the prime rate. That means that when the interest rate for big-business borrowing goes down, it usually goes down for us, too.

$ Will you give them anything you already own that they can keep if you don't pay them back?
If you give lenders something valuable they can keep, they feel better about lending. If you don't pay—that's called a *default,* in Moneytalk—they keep

the item, sell it, and get their money anyway. So if you have something valuable to put up for a loan, called *collateral*, in Moneytalk, you can borrow money cheaper than if you don't.

Can you guess the two main things that grown-ups put up as collateral? *That's right. Their house and their car.*

How to Shop for Money

You can see that money can be borrowed expensively or cheaply. If you need to borrow, you want the interest to be as low as possible. You can shop around for money just the way you do for toys.

Shopping for money is called *comparing interest rates.* Here is how it works:

Let's say you want to borrow $10.00. The lender will say, "Our interest rate is 5 percent." (No matter how much you need to borrow, the cost is always expressed in a percentage.) Of course, 5 percent of $10.00 is $0.50. So when you pay back the money, the lender gets $10.50.

Let's say you used the money to buy clothes. The store-keeper sells you $10.00 worth of clothes, but you have to pay the lender $10.50. That's why things bought with borrowed money are always more expensive than things bought with saved money. You end up having to work harder and save longer to pay the lender than to buy the thing itself.

Here are some of the places that you can go to borrow money:

$ Stores will lend you money to buy their stuff.
$ Credit card companies will give you a borrowing card.
$ Banks will give you loans with and without collateral.

You shop for credit by comparing the interest rates they charge. Here are some real-life examples:

The Plastic Flash: Credit Cards

A *credit card* is a plastic card that allows you to buy stuff without paying for it right away. The companies, such as American Express, VISA, MasterCard, Diner's Card, Discover Card, and many others, lend you money to buy the items you want.

Credit card loans are easy to get, but the interest rate is high. I bet you know why the cost of using a credit card is higher than the cost of other credit. It's because:

$ There is no collateral.
$ The loan is small.
$ It's for a short period of time.

If you don't pay up the amount you borrow every month exactly on time, you get charged an interest rate of up to 20 percent. That means that what you bought costs 20 percent more than it would have if you paid with a check or cash.

Spend-and-Save Cards

Today, there is a new type of card called *spend-and-save*. For every dollar you spend, you get a refund or another type of bonus at the store where you made the purchase. I can't decide about these cards. Of course, it's nice to get money back if you are going to buy something. But it also may convince you to buy something you don't need, like a sale does sometimes. In the end, the best thing to do, in my opinion, is to use the spend-and-save card if you were going to buy the item anyway but not get sucked into buying what you don't want in the first place.

How do you feel about credit cards? This is my view:

Would Use For:	Would Not Use For:
Furniture over $150	Ball game tickets
Meals (keep receipts)	Toys
Clothes over $30	Luxuries like a stereo
Out-of-state purchases	Fast food

My view is to use cards to keep good records, for things that will last a long time, and for convenience. As you can see, sometimes credit is good to use, but sometimes you can get into trouble. Being able to tell the difference is very important.

17

Borrowing and a Kid's Future

Credit is like a tool that helps you build fast.

When Borrowing Is No Good

They say that the U.S. government is in so much debt that we kids will have to pay for it all our lives. What they mean is that when we pay our taxes, which you'll read about in Chapter 21, a lot of the money will go to pay for old things bought by the government for our parents instead of new things that we need. An example is roads and bridges. By the time we need new ones, our tax dollars may be going to pay the debt on old ones built years ago.

Even worse, some of the things that governments and people buy disappear. *Unlike roads and bridges, spending money on silly things is a real waste.* Sometimes people and governments spend money wastefully. This becomes very bad when they have to borrow the money

But...if you use too much credit, it can destroy all you have.

they waste. It means that for years they pay back money used for things that did them no good in the first place.

So we can pretty much agree that using *credit,* also called borrowing money, is no good when:

$ The interest rates are high, and the money is expensive to get

$ The thing you buy with it disappears fast, and the only thing left is the debt you have to pay back

$ You don't have enough income to make the payments and you have to default

When you don't pay, you can lose your collateral or get sued. Worst of all, you end up with a bad credit rating. That means that the next time you ask to borrow, the lender will charge you more money in interest to make up for your bad creditworthiness.

But sometimes borrowing money can work well and get you just what you want. Borrowing money can be just what you need to be a success.

Totally Awesome Ways of Borrowing Money

By borrowing money, you can buy and own investments much faster than if you saved up from your income. When you use the very thing that you are buying as collateral for the loan you are taking to buy it, this is called *leverage*, in Moneytalk. Leverage, the ability to use as collateral the thing you want to buy on borrowed money, is a way of increasing your success as an investor. For example, when you get older and are investing in stocks, you can open a special account that allows you to borrow money from the brokerage firms to buy stocks. You can borrow up to 50 percent of the value of the stocks you have in your stock account. In Moneytalk, this is called *buying on margin*.

Buying a House

The best example of how leverage works is buying a house. If your parents own their own home, I bet that they used leverage to buy it. If they did, that was a good type of borrowing, not a bad one. Here's how it works:

Let's say your mom and dad have $20,000 to buy a house. Maybe they saved it by making a budget. Perhaps it took 5 years to save all that money. Now you are born, and they need more room or a neighborhood with a good school.

So now they go shopping for a house. Wow! Prices are

high. The house they like costs $80,000. If it took them 5 years to save $20,000, it could take them another 15 years to save the rest.

They decide to borrow $60,000 to pay for the house and buy it right away. Luckily, a bank, the seller of the house, or another lender agrees to lend them the money provided they put up the house they will buy as collateral.

In other words, if your parents default (don't pay), the lender can take the house back. When your parents finish paying the loan, they own the house free and clear. The right of the lender to take the house back if payment is not made is on record in the county clerk's office where you live. The paper that gets recorded is called a *mortgage*, in Moneytalk.

This is a totally cool way of borrowing money. Look at all the good it does:

$ Your mom and dad get to buy a house years earlier than they could by saving.

$ You get to live in it and enjoy it.

$ Eventually, they pay off the mortgage, and they own the house with no debt.

$ Believe it or not, the government gives them a tax break for taking the loan. (You'll read about that in Chapter 21.)

How Leverage Makes You Money

Here is the best part. This is why leverage is more than cool, it is awesome! Let's say your mom and dad decide to sell the house before they pay off the mortgage. Maybe they found a house that they like better or one of them wants to move to get a better job. Even though they used the house as collateral, they can still sell it.

Let's say it is now worth $90,000. The price went up because of the nice things your folks did to fix it up. It's worth more now than when they bought it. All they have to pay back is the amount they borrowed. They can pay that from the sale price of the house. Guess what! They get to keep the extra $10,000 as a profit. That's a pretty good investment.

Leverage for Math Brains

Here's something for math brains. If your folks paid the whole $80,000 and did not take a loan but used cash, how much of a percentage did they make on their investment if they sold for $90,000? Answer: 12.5 percent. (The profit of $10,000 is 12.5 percent of $80,000.)

Since your folks did borrow and put only $20,000 into the house, how much of a percentage did they make if they sold the house at the same $90,000? Answer: 50 percent. (The profit of $10,000 is 50 percent of $20,000.)

In the first case, they made a 12.5 percent profit. Cool! In the second case, they made a 50 percent profit. Awesome!

You can use leverage to buy lots of things: a business, a stock, art. But remember, try to pick something that will have the same or higher value in the future, or you can be left with a debt instead of a profit.

The Leverage Game

Each player starts at Start. The first player chooses from one to four dice to throw at each turn. For every die the players choose, they are down 5 points. But they get to move the number of spaces that the total throw gives them. They then win or lose the points indicated on the space in which they landed.

So a player can leverage his or her turn (that is, increase its power) by using more dice. Naturally, with leverage, the player also

takes the extra risk of throwing less than a 5 with any of the dice chosen. Since each die "costs" 5 points to use, it's important that the return be a 5 or more to help the player win.

In real investing, leverage also helps you make money faster, so in our game, there are extra points for the player who comes in first, no matter what his or her game point total is by the end of the game. The first to end the game wins 100 points; the second 75 points; the third 50 points.

Play the game five times, and the one with the most game and speed points wins.

What kind of player are you? Do you like to take the risk and leverage your turn, or do you play it slow and safe?

+10	+10	+10		-10	+15	+15
-5		-10		+10		-15
-5		-10		+10		-20
+5		+10		-10		-5
+5		+5		+5		+5
+5		+5		+5		+10
+5		+5		+5		+15
+5		-5		-5		+20
+5		-5		-10		0
START		+10	+10	-10		END

Part 4

MONEY AND REAL LIFE

"Do what you love. The money will follow."*
—Irwin Earner

*Title of a great book by Marsha Sinetar

Of course, all money matters have to do with real life. But there are some things that we have to do almost every day that relate to money. One of them is to work and get paid. It's no fun to pick a job just to make money. When I'm grown up, I sure hope I pick work I love to do.

But most kids work just to get paid. They need some extra money, so they deliver groceries or have a paper route. I may do that, but right now I like the idea of being in business, even a kid's business like offering to manage a blockwide garage sale in return for 5 percent of the profits.

Whatever way you make money, you have to know what to charge and make sure you get paid. It's not easy when the people who give you the money are not your family. It's business, not love. It's real life.

Another real-life money chore is paying bills. How often has your mom and dad said, "I'm the one who pays the bills around here." Wow, bill paying doesn't sound like much fun. In writing this book, I spent time with my mother while she paid bills. It was very tiring watching her write out all those checks. But that's part of real life, too. So let's learn some of these things.

18
Money and Work

*"When you work,
you trade this for this."*

Most of our money will come from the work we do each day. That means we exchange the time of our life for money.

When you look for any job, be sure that you really want it and that you think you would be good at it. Once you are hired, be clear about what you are supposed to do. If you are working for someone, get a job description. Try to sit down before your first day of work and actually write down what is expected of you as explained by the employer. Show him or her what you think the job is about. This helps a lot as the job goes on. It also makes you less confused and nervous about starting out. If you are offering a service or in other ways working at your own business, you should also have an understanding with your customers.

Here are some basic things to do:

$ If you have a job now, write down what you think is expected of you. See what your parents think of how you describe your job.

$ Have a clear and definite deal. Before work is started, know when and how much you will be paid.

$ Please the boss. Do a good job. Pay attention to the extra things the boss needs, and try to do them.

Send a bill. Here's an example:

```
Invoice Dated May 2, 1993
   RE: Lawn mowing at 1705 Maple Road for
       the week of April 25—May 2
       $20.00                      Balance Due
   Please Pay Immediately
   Late Charge $0.25 Per Week
```

Get a Raise

After you have worked for a while, it máy be time to ask for a raise. Maybe you have already made a deal to get one by a certain date. But if you haven't, you'll have to ask.

Sometimes that's hard to do because you'll feel bad if the boss says no. Here are some hints to make it easier:

$ Don't think the boss won't like you if you ask.

$ Don't ask when the boss is busy.

$ Know how much of a raise you want.

$ If the boss says no, ask for a little less.

$ If the boss still says no, say, "OK, we will talk about it again next month." And bring it up again.

The super-easiest way to get a raise is to think of something extra to do for the boss that you see he or she needs.

Doing something for others is the best way to get something back for yourself.

If you are already doing any kind of work, what are some things you notice that are not getting done? Are they things you can do? Can you get extra pay?

How Hard Is It for You to Ask for Money or a Raise?

Answer these questions for yourself. There is no right or wrong answer.

- $ Do you feel awkward asking for a raise?
- $ How much more do you want?
- $ Is the amount based on what others earn? How did you pick the figure?
- $ Do you feel you are doing a good job?
- $ How will you feel if your boss says no?
- $ Are you on good terms with your boss?

If you feel undeserving or ashamed to ask for money, you probably won't get paid what you are worth. Once you understand your own feelings, you can practice asking.

A Word About Jobs

I do not have a job (except for writing this book). But I am always thinking of ways to be self-employed. Most kids are self-employed because the child labor laws forbid us to be hired on a regular basis. There are many ways that we can earn money anyway. Here are a few of them:

- $ Try putting up a lemonade stand.
- $ Try something I've tried: Collect leaves and other

things from your backyard, make compost, and sell it as fertilizer.

$ Buy ice at your local grocery store, crush it, and pour different types of juices on it. Guess what? You've made a slushy. Sell them in front of your home.

There are many ups and downs to being self-employed. Here are some of the pros: You will never have to ask your boss for a raise, because you are the boss. That's what self-employed means. You are your own boss. And you can make your own hours.

Now, some cons: Some people when they are self-employed tend to be loose with themselves. They don't keep strict rules about their business, and then they tend to lose money because they don't pay attention. So, don't get carried away with yourself.

Things to Do
Ask your mom and dad about their first jobs.

$ **Was it a summer job?**
$ **What did they do?**
$ **How much were they paid?**
$ **What did they do with the money they earned?**
$ **How old were they?**

Ask your grandparents the same questions. Ask other members of your family, like your older brother and/or sister. Ask yourself. Compare the answers and see how times change. Or do they?

1ST JOB   HOW OLD   PAID   What did they do with the money?
Me
Mom

Dad

Grandpa

Grandma

Older brother

Older sister

Other

What Would You Do If...?

How would you handle these tough on-the-job problems?

1. The man whose lawn you mow offers you $5 extra to cross a busy street and buy him groceries. It's not part of your job, and your mom doesn't want you to cross the street.
2. You work in a store at the cash register. A customer gives you too much money by mistake and starts to walk out the door.
3. Your boss tells you "Times are tough" and wants you to take less money to do the same job.
4. The lemonade stand across the street charges less money than you do but doesn't use healthy stuff. They get more business.

There are lots of approaches to all these problems above. Here are a few:

1. Don't go. Politely say your mom won't like it, and she may make you quit. Tell him that since you enjoy mowing the lovely lawn, you would hate to have to leave the job.
2. Call the customer back, and give him his change. Money gotten the wrong way never does you any good for long.

3. If you like your job, or if other jobs are hard to find, offer to do any extra chores for the same pay. If it doesn't work, offer to work for less for two weeks and then review the situation. Meanwhile, look around for other jobs.

4. It's time to advertise. Let everyone know they get what they pay for.

A Word About Allowances

You'd think that in a book about money for kids, there would be tons of stuff about allowances. Get real. A study showed that most kids get a $2 allowance, and that hasn't changed in years.

Most kids just get money in a helter-skelter way, or they

nag their folks for stuff. Up until you are a teenager, that's not so bad. Where do you and your family stand in the allowance picture?

$ When was the last time you got an increase?

$ Who decides if you should get one now?

$ Do you keep a budget? Do a budget and show it to your parents to get the increase. They'll be impressed.

$ If you don't have a budget, do you feel you need one?

$ How do you get stuff? Do your parents buy it? Do your grandparents give you gifts?

$ Do you get enough stuff?

$ Does your brother or sister get more?

$ Do you have a problem with fairness?

To talk to your parents about unfairness or a need you have, use what you learned about wishes, goals, and plans earlier in this book. If you have a goal, your parents may help you reach it. If you just want more stuff, they will probably say no.

Let the whole family give their views on allowances.

DANIEL'S ALLOWANCE

Daniel was fifteen years old and did not get an allowance. But his parents bought him everything that he wanted or needed. They bought him games and food, and they also gave him money for going out with his friends.

One day during dinner, Daniel's parents asked him a question: "Which would you rather have? That we buy you all the things that you need, or that we give you $25 allowance a week?"

Daniel wasn't sure what to choose. He thought all through dinner. At the end of dinner, he had an answer. He chose to have his parents buy him everything that he needed. He decided that because $25 might not cover his expenses, and then he would be in trouble. Daniel wasn't prepared for the goal setting and budgeting it takes to manage an allowance.

Which would you have chosen, and why? What can Daniel's parents do to make him more independent and feel more capable of money management?

19
Paying Bills

"Pay on time and avoid late charges."
—Pablo Payment

Most of the time, a kid spends money on the spot. But sometimes, you buy something that you pay for later on, usually at the end of the month. The person you pay sends a bill, like the one you may send for your work. These bills are all part of your expenses and should be in your budget.

Once a month you pay your bills. Some of them are tax deductible (see Chapter 21), so you need to keep records. Others aren't, but you need to keep a record of payment in case someone says you did not pay. Typical bills that most grown-ups and some kids pay are:

- $ Telephone bill
- $ Fuel bill
- $ Credit card bill
- $ Mortgage
- $ Light bill, called *utility*

The best way to keep track and to make payments is to pay by check.

You can open a checking account with your bank. Most of these accounts don't pay interest, and they are not investments. They are for convenience, record keeping, and safety in bill paying.

As proof that you have money in your checking account, the bank will give you a checkbook. Every time you write out a check, you must deduct the amount from the balance in the account. In Moneytalk, this is called *balancing the checkbook*. Grown-ups make a big deal about this. Here's why:

$ If the math is wrong and you write checks for more than the money in the account, the bank charges a big penalty.

$ If the bank makes a math mistake, it's a pain to get it corrected.

$ If you forget to write down and deduct an amount you wrote, you get *overdrawn*.

So this is the simplest way I found to balance your checkbook. I learned it from my fifth-grade teacher, Ms. Delaney, at the Maplewood Middle School in Maplewood, New Jersey.

How to Balance a Checkbook

Balancing a checkbook is very important to good banking and to general money management. Before learning about balancing a checkbook, take a good look at a check.

1. Who are you making the check out to? Write down his or her or a company's name. If you make it out to "Cash," it means that you are making it out to

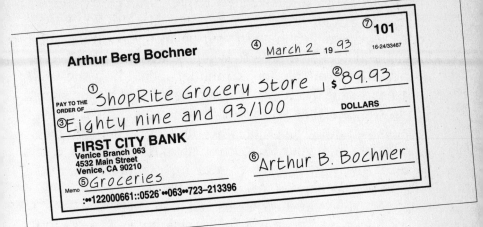

anyone who gets ahold of the check.

2. The amount of the check is written in numbers. This is the amount that will be deducted from your checking account and the amount the recipient will get from a bank when it is deposited.

3. The amount of the check written in words.

4. The date the check is made out is written in.

5. This is the *memo,* a note to yourself about what you are paying for. In this case, it is groceries. It could be baby-sitting, or any service or product. If you are paying a bill, write the bill number here. You will find it on the *invoice.* See Chapter 18.

6. Add your signature. The check is not good without it.

7. This is the check number. This helps you keep good records and prove you paid if someone says you didn't.

Balancing a checkbook is easy once you get the hang of it. Here's an example:

Let's say that you have $1,000 in your checking account.

You go to Shoprite for groceries. The bill comes out to $89.93, so you decide to pay by check. Before you write your check, you should go to your balance sheet. First you fill in the date. Then note to whom you wrote the check; then write down the check number located on the top right-hand side. Then you will see a plus and minus sign. Circle the one that you want; in this case, it's a minus because you are giving money to the store. Then subtract your $89.93 from your $1,000. You get $910.07; this is your balance. Always write your checks in pen and fill out your book in pen. When you make a deposit, do the exact same thing, but circle the plus sign instead of the minus.

Checks are a great way to pay bills, but you must keep track of the account balance. If you don't, the bank will

Date	Number	To / From	Amount / Balance	
3/2/93	101	ShopRite groceries	+ Ⓜ 89.93	
			910.07	
3/3/93	102	Toys 'R' Us Nintendo	+ Ⓜ 30.00	
			880.07	
3/4/93	X	Boss - John Smith Paycheck	Ⓜ - 300.00	
			1180.07	
3/5/93	103	Boys Electronics Radio	+ Ⓜ 150.00	
			1030.07	
3/6/93	104	United Airlines Plane Tickets- L.A.	+ Ⓜ 139.00	
			891.07	
3/7/93	105	Hilton Hotels Suite/ room service	+ Ⓜ 120.00	
			771.07	

refuse to give the money to the recipient and will also charge you a fee. This is called *bouncing a check*. It will embarrass you, cost you money, and annoy the person who expects to get paid. It also hurts your credit and ability to borrow in the future.

Riddle

Q. Why is a baseball fly-out like a good check?

A. Neither of them bounces.

Part 5

MONEY MATTERS FOR OLDER KIDS

MARS UNIVERSITY

Things are different for the class of 2003.

Last year, I was allowed to attend a business camp that is part of The Foundation for Free Enterprise because my mom taught there. Most of the other kids were fifteen years old. All of them were really worried about going to college. I've been hearing about college and its cost for as long as I can remember.

For some kids, college time is right around the corner. I gather from what I hear, especially from questions at my mother's lectures, that times have changed a lot. When our parents were college age, it was much cheaper than it is today. Parents all seem very concerned about costs.

"You're never too young to pay taxes."

Chapter 20 will give you information on getting aid, grants, and scholarships. That's pretty important for the older kids. Age fifteen is the right time to look into these things.

And whether you go to college or not, as long as you make any money you'll have to pay your taxes. In fact, I learned that starting at age fourteen a kid gets his or her own tax bracket. Right now, my tax bracket is the same as my parents', but it won't be for long. I'll be a taxpayer before I can drive or vote!

20
Getting to College

"I'm glad my money know-how paid off."
—Arnold Almost Adult

One of the biggest worries on a lot of kids' minds is getting to college.. It's very expensive.

For example, when I am ready to go in seven years, four years of college will cost over $100,000 for a private school and over $50,000 for a public school. If I think about that long enough, it looks like there is no chance. I'd have to invest $576 every month to get to public college and $1,261 to get to a private school. No way for a kid, and no way for my parents either. And that's if I could lend my money and get 8 percent. No wonder the whole country is in a panic about getting us to college.

But I was determined to give you a solution in this book. So after looking at a lot of materials, I have one very good thing to report: *Anyone who wants to go to college can, no matter how much money he or she has.* None of us are going to prance into a college and pay with pocket change. Still, there are opportunities if you know how to find them.

Don't Let the Numbers Scare You

When our parents were our age, college was a lot cheaper. Mostly, if they got good grades, they could go. So they think that college tuition should grow on trees, that everyone must go from high school to college and live in fancy dorms. But this old approach is very expensive and may be impossible for us. When I looked at the numbers, this is what I discovered:

Only half the money goes for tuition in a public school and 75 percent in a private school. About 5 percent goes for books and labs. The rest goes for room and board. (*Board* means food.) About 15 percent goes for food. That means that if we choose where we live carefully and don't go overboard on a big lifestyle, we can save some costs.

In the bibliography, there is a list of books just on getting to college. They have great ideas that will appeal to you. But most important, we can think in a new way about getting to college.

My Top Five Best Bets for Getting to College

1. *Get all the information you can by the time you are fifteen.* Here's what to do: Go to your high school's guidance office, and get their material on loans, grants, scholarships, and other aid. Go to the financial aid offices at the colleges you like, and get their aid information. Look up your local U.S. Department of Education office in the phone book and ask for their materials. Really read this material together with the books listed in the bibliography to learn every way you can get money for college. This is a full-year project at least. Start early.

2. *Get a Stafford Loan.* This is a government loan we all can get no matter how much money our folks have. You can get up to $17,125 this way. *Get a Pell Grant.* If our parents' income is below $42,000, you can get $3,700 a year for college.

3. *Get an associate's degree first.* You can go to a two-year college, which is much less expensive, then shift into a four-year college, and end up with the same degree for almost half price. This works because the four-year college will accept all or most of the credits you have already accumulated.

4. *Join the Army.* You can join the armed services and get a free college education.

5. *Look for a work-study program.* This way you can pay your own way through college and get important job experience, too.

What to Do with the Money Your Parents Saved for College

Some of us have money set aside for college by our parents, grandparents, or other people who care. A lot of my friends don't know how much is saved for them. I think it's OK to ask about it, but don't be surprised if your folks don't want to tell you. Maybe they think you'll want the money for something else or that they will have to use it in an emergency and you'll be disappointed.

Whether they talk to you about your college nest egg or not, I found out a few things that you can say to them that will help everyone out:

$ *Find out if you can prepay tuition.* Some private colleges will let you prepay the tuition at any age. If you don't go, you get your money back. Since tuition is slated to increase each year, you can pay for school in 2020 at today's cost.

$ *Find out if your state has a prepayment plan.* A few states will also let you prepay the public school costs. This can be a real bargain.

$ *Remind your folks that 35 percent of your savings is counted if you apply for aid, but that only 5.6 percent of their savings is counted.* Lots of folks think it's nice to put the money in the kid's name, but this can actually hurt your chances for aid.

Finally, by the time you are fifteen, work with your parents to learn all the rules. Be flexible about your goals, and then make plans. While there's not much that we younger kids can do to help out, it doesn't hurt to get good grades and to tell our parents that college is important to us (if it is).

21
Now That You Have Made Some Money, It's Time to Pay Your Taxes

"Now that I've got money it's time to pay taxes."

—Irwin Earner

Taxes are money that a government collects from its citizens to use to run the government. In the United States, we pay taxes according to how much income we make every year. April 15 is tax day. It is our responsibility to file a tax return that shows what we earned from work and investments. We then reduce this total amount by any expenses or other money that the law lets us deduct from our earnings. Then, we use a tax table to calculate our tax. Finally, we pay.

The U.S. Government's Totally Awesome Tax System

What is so amazing about our tax system is that it is voluntary. We fill out our own forms, do our own math, and send in the money to the tax collector. If we want to, we can instruct our employers to send some of our money to the tax collector as we get paid during the year. This is called *tax withholding*, and it makes it easier to pay up when the time comes. Depending on how many dependents you tell the employer you have, he or she will withhold more or less from your paychecks. Having more dependents results in less money being withheld.

Some people don't pay, don't fill out the form correctly, or don't pay the right amount. When this happens, the tax collector has the right to review the taxpayer's papers. This is called an *audit*. If the taxpayer is thought wrong by the tax collector, he or she may have to pay a fine or a penalty. Still, there is a Taxpayer's Bill of Rights that allows a taxpayer to take the case to a court and to have the audit in a convenient place. And it gives other kinds of protection from abuse.

Who Is the Tax Collector?

The tax collector is called the *Internal Revenue Service (IRS)*. The tax law is called the *Internal Revenue Code*.

How Much Tax Will You Pay?

The amount of taxes you pay is based on two things: (1) the amount of money you made during the year and (2) the money you can deduct from it before you must figure out your final tax. Federal taxes, the biggest tax of all, changed recently. For now you pay 15 percent of the first $20,350 you earn (that's $3,052.50), 28 percent of the next $28,950 you earn (that's $8,106), and 31 percent of the next amount you earn, whatever that is. Married couples pay a little differently. But pretty soon the highest bracket will be up to 39.6 percent. And new tax laws may change all these percentages soon.

As for the things you can deduct, there are so many it's hard to make a list. Here are some important ones:

$ Expenses related to making money, such as travel, stationery, and secretarial pay
$ The cost of doctors and medicine if you are sick
$ Other taxes (except sales taxes) you paid to the state in which you live or for the land taxes on your house
$ Interest that you paid to the bank if you have a mortgage

How to Pay the Right Amount of Tax

Under the Taxpayer's Bill of Rights, every citizen is allowed to pay as little tax as is legitimately possible. That's why the super-most important thing you should do to save on taxes is keep good records. After all, it's not possible to take all the deductions if you can't remember what you spent. Every time you forget to take a deduction or you can't prove it to the IRS, you lose money.

Investing to Save Taxes

There are many ways that you can save taxes by choosing tax-safe investments.

Taxed Never

One way to save taxes is to invest in municipal bonds. These are loans you make to a city or state in return for interest payments (see Chapter 8). Because of the Constitution of the United States, the federal government can't tax you on money you have earned from lending to state or city governments. It would be unconstitutional.

The reason that the signers of the Constitution wanted to prevent the government from taxing loans made to it by us is that they thought such taxes would be a way for the federal government to keep the states poor and take over their power.

Taxed Later

A different kind of tax-wise investment is called *tax deferral,* in Moneytalk. There are certain kinds of accounts in which you can keep your money and investments that don't get counted when they make money for you—until you actually take the money out. The word *deferred* is really just a fancy way of saying *delayed* or *later.*

You do get taxed on the money you make in these special accounts, but not until later on, in the year when you use the money. Meanwhile, the earnings and profits keep getting reinvested without any taxes taken out. This makes a big difference in how much you end up with. For example, if you invested $2,000 every year, earning 9 percent interest in the 31 percent tax bracket, at the end of twenty-five years you would have $184,648 if the investment was tax deferred, $120,049 if it was not deferred.

The cool thing is that even kids can use these special tax-deferred accounts. Many people don't know that. If you earn money, you can put up to $2,000 a year in an account called an *IRA,* or *individual retirement account.* That's what I did with the money I made from this book.

The Kiddie Tax: No Kidding

Don't think that just because you are a kid you don't have to pay taxes. You do. There is a *kiddie tax* (I hate that phrase). And it doesn't matter how young you are, as long as you earn money from work or make money from investing. You've seen those little babies in the tire commercials on TV. They get paid for jumping around in diapers, and they have to pay an income tax just like bigger kids. They get their own tax bracket, and their parents or a guardian has to file a tax return for them.

But if a kid has money from profits or interest, not from working, there is a different rule. Here is how that kiddie tax works:

For money you earn by investing (not from work), up to the time you are fourteen you pay the same percentage of your income as your parents pay of theirs. The percentage of your income that you must pay in taxes is called your *tax bracket*, in Moneytalk. So if your parents pay 15 percent, so do you.

Once you reach age fourteen, you get your own tax bracket. Probably you don't make much, so you'll be in the 15 percent bracket.

If you earn money from work, you get your own tax bracket right away. Most of us kids don't have to worry too much because the first $1,200 we earn is not taxed. Not a lot of kids earn more than that. If you do, your parents are probably filling out kiddie tax forms for you. They sign them as your guardian. Gee, we're old enough to pay taxes but not old enough to sign our own forms. Bummer!

Final Note: How You Feel About Money Says a Lot About You

As I wrote this book, my mom kept saying, "Money is a neutral thing. It's not good or bad. It's all according to how you feel and think about it." As with many things, not everyone agrees about money matters. Maybe your folks fight about money with each other, with your brother or sister, or with you. Maybe your friends have different ideas. That's no surprise. Money is a big topic, and people feel differently about it.

What I learned about money in writing this book is that developing a money style and handling money are part of growing up. Dealing with feelings about money is also part of growing up. How you work things out says a lot about your future career, life choices, and even happiness.

When Keith, my editor, asked me to write a final chapter for the book, I looked through it to pick out the things I wanted to think more about.

Goals: What Are Yours?

People have different goals. Some are short term; others are long term. One may be to go to college; another might be to be a senator or a lawyer. My goal in life is to be a paleobotanist. That's a long-term goal. However, I also have a short-term goal. It is to go to the best college for aspiring scientists. This is where the money comes in. By now, *you* have had time to think about *your* goals.

Do You Have a Plan to Reach Your Goals?

To achieve a goal, you must have a plan. A plan is something that will get you somewhere or get you something. Here is an example of a goal: I want to go to college, and I need to save money to do it. Here is my plan: I will do more odd jobs around the house, and I will mow more front lawns every week. When I get the extra money, I will put it in the bank. Before long I'm on my way.

Budgets: A Look at Thomas

Many people have a budget. But others don't like them. A budget is a thing that will help you organize and make a plan. Remember Thomas? He used a budget to help him get some things that he wanted. What do you want your budget to do for you?

Money in Your Future

How important do you think money will be to you? Just because we know about money and how to invest it doesn't mean that it has to rule our lives. Will money be prominent in your life? What kind of grown-up do you think you will be as far as money is concerned?

What Do You Consider Financial Success?

When will you be happy with how much money you have? That's one of the biggest questions that grown-ups have to answer. My mother read a study that said that all the adults polled wanted double the money that they had or double the money that they earned. When I heard this, I was very surprised. I always thought that adults had a lot of contentment with what they have. Obviously not. How much money do you think you will need to earn each year to be content?

Collector, Trader, or Buyer—Which Are You?

A collector is a person who accumulates things like baseball cards, comic books, coins, or anything that will be worth something later. Then he or she sells part of it once in a while to get better stuff. A trader is a person who's just like a collector; but instead of buying things to trade up, he or she buys to make money. A buyer is a person who will buy the things just as the trader or collector would but will not sell them. He or she is a keeper. What are you? A buyer, a trader, or a collector?

Socially Responsible Investing: What Do You Believe In?

Socially responsible investing means that you invest in a company that you believe does things the right way. For instance, you might think that testing products on animals is not right, so you won't invest in companies that test on animals. What are some socially responsible things that are important to you?

Taxes: Do You Think They Are Fair?

Taxes are something that everybody has to pay. You pay them to the federal and state governments every year on April 15 if you make money from working or investments.

Taxes are very high. As much as 44 percent of every dollar you earn may go to taxes, depending on the tax rates of the state in which you live. You keep the rest. They say that the average person works from January to May just to pay taxes. You pay taxes on many other things, like the property and the house that you own and the things that you buy. Taxes are collected so the government can spend money on things that are good for everyone. What are some of the things you think the government should spend your tax money on? When you are old enough to vote, elect people who agree with you about this.

Hey, Kids, This Part Is Just Between You and Me

This is the second time that I have written to you personally about this book. This time, it is about how much you have learned throughout the book. I hope you have learned many things that will help you in your life. But there is only one way to find out: *Take a test.*

I had to fight with Keith, my editor, and my mom to keep this test in the book. They think that tests are boring and that mine will scare you away. They forget that in school we get tests with breakfast, lunch, and dinner. Bored is our middle name. So what could one more little test hurt, to see how much you know about money? At least there is no teacher grading you on it.

1. When you look for a loan, are high interest rates good for you?

2. If you wanted to buy a stock, why would you want to know its P/E ratio?

3. If you want to buy a $150,000 house but you only have $60,000, what could you do?

4. What does DRIP stand for?

5. What happens to the prices of things when the government puts a tax on them? Name things that you buy that have a tax on them.

6. What is dollar cost averaging?

7. Is a mutual fund a group of stocks or a single

stock?

8. How does the government tax children's income? Earnings from investments? Does it make a difference how old you are?

9. What does a broker do?

10. How is it possible to invest your money in a foreign country?

You probably don't know the answers to all these questions. But if you got any right, that's great. All the answers are in the book, and as you do more, read more, and learn more about money, it will all come easily.

Well, enjoy your financial life, and, most of all, have fun.

Mom Gets the Last Word

Dear Parents,

Financial success need not mean great wealth or riches. Most of us are happiest with lifelong feelings of security and prosperity. Lately, it seems these feelings have eluded us. How we face our money challenges and opportunities often has more to do with our childhood experiences than our adult circumstances.

Why do some people bounce back from financial adversity to become even stronger? Why do others continually fail to make ends meet? Inner resources, coping skills, and attitudes toward money are all learned. There is nothing genetic about money except the accident of inheritance.

But as parents, when we throw the ball to our kids, it's hard to know where they will run with it. Whether we realize it or not, we are teaching our child about money. We do it by example, in our casual conversations, and in our inevitable money fights. Every time we choose a gift, give a party, or go to the movies, we have a spending event that reveals a little of our "money self" to our kids.

What our children absorb is the family money culture that forms the basis of their reaction system. You won't be surprised to learn that what you do and say has more influence on your children's response to earning, saving, investing, and thinking about money than anything else.

For instance, it can be very telling to ask your child which are the happiest families he or she knows. Find a point of reference familiar to your child. Arthur watches TV a great deal (tsk, tsk), so he knows all the TV families. Maybe you would prefer to use book references or ones from real life. In any case, pick a few, making sure to include some that are obviously rich and poor.

Next, ask your child to associate some of these attributes with each: organized, friendly, safe, happy, loving, neat, jolly, cross, loud, sweet. You'd be surprised how often the blue-collar family in "Roseanne" wins, over the affluent family in "Growing Pains," and how often the impoverished *Five Little Peppers* do better than the wealthy kids in *The Secret Garden.*

Unlike other topics, even sex and drugs, we rarely talk to our kids about money directly. Mostly, they learn by example and innuendo. "What kind of money baby were you?" is a question I often ask in the books I write for adults. How are your kids interpreting what they hear about work, money, and investing in the home?

How to Discuss Family Money Culture

I have ended this book with two exercises that you can do with your children informally to help you find out. The first is a list of money sayings that your children hear in the home, mostly from you. You can add to the list. Then you can talk to them about what they think the sayings mean.

My purpose is to give you a method of learning how your children are developing with regard to their money personalities without asking directly. No child can tell you if he or she is a saver or spender. But your children can tell you that Grandma keeps saying, "We never were allowed to have that when I was your age," and how it makes them feel.

You can ask kids how they feel about things they hear about money and our economy in the news, in school, on TV, and in the home. Any time we get a better understanding of how our actions and the actions of others affect our kids, we can better direct them.

The second exercise is your financial family tree. Arthur knows who his ancestors were, when they immigrated to the United States, how political oppression in Europe forced them to relinquish their assets, and how each generation rebuilt.

This understanding makes him proud even though he is not the richest guy in town. Kids don't think too much about money and status until the world forces them to do so. I believe that family pride will help them see through false values better than any direct teaching from us.

Do you hear any of these money phrases at home? If so, who in your family says them? What do you think they mean? How do they make you feel?

$ "He's money mad."

$ "He's only out for money."

$ "Money isn't everything."

$ "She's lucky; she doesn't have to work."

$ "Money doesn't grow on trees."

$ "Money makes money."

$ "I can never understand anything about money."

$ "I've been rich, and I've been poor. Rich is better."

Family Financial Tree

Here is a good discussion for a child to have with his mom and dad and an even better one to have with his grandparents.

Have your child find out if your family or any of your ancestors were rich, poor, landowners, even royalty. Here are questions he or she might want to ask.

$ Where did my great-grandparents come from? My grandparents?

$ What kind of house did they live in?

$ Did the family's fortunes ever change because of wars, bad business, or other troubles?

$ What did my great-grandparents and grandparents do for a living?

$ Are there any good stories about how a family member made lots of money?

Oh, yes. Even if the kids know about money, they won't confuse rich with happy. Only grown-ups do that. Just ask them.

Glossary

Accountant: A professional who helps you with your tax return and other tax tasks.

Banker: One who works in a bank lending money and investing your deposits, securities (stocks), or bonds.

Borrowing: Using someone else's money with their permission in return for giving it back to them, sometimes with extra money for letting you use theirs.

Broker: One licensed to buy and sell stocks for you.

Budget: A way of keeping track of money you get and spend.

Call: The money you lent is paid back early. This can happen with a bond.

Capital: The amount of money you invest.

Collateral: Stuff you will have to forfeit to someone who lends you money if you can't pay them back.

Collectibles: Items that you buy, such as baseball cards or art, with the idea of selling them someday for more than you paid.

Commission: A percentage of the cost of an investment you made that you pay to a broker for buying the investment for you. To buy some investments, you need a special license, so you can't buy them yourself.

Commodities: Anything that is traded, like agricultural products, gold, and oil, in the belief that it will be worth more later and can be sold to make money.

There are three major differences between collectibles

and commodities: (1) You usually like what you collect; commodities are not important to you except to make money. (2) You usually take what you collect home; a broker just keeps a record of the commodities you buy. (3) You own collectibles for a long time; when you decide to sell, it takes awhile to find a buyer. Commodities are bought and sold fast; there is always a quick market for selling through a broker.

Company: A business.

Credit: The ability to borrow money.

Debt: The obligation to pay back borrowed money.

Default: Not paying back the money you borrowed.

Discount Broker: One who charges lower commissions or charges you based on the number of shares you buy, not their price.

Diversification: Investing in many different things to reduce your risk of loss overall.

Dollar Cost Averaging: Investing the same amount of money every period so as to do better than if you invested a lot at once.

DRIP (Dividend Reinvestment Plan): Automatically buys more shares of stock with profits.

Emerging Growth Countries: Countries that are just beginning to have economies that you can invest in.

Expenses: Your cost of living.

FDIC (Federal Deposit Insurance Corporation): An agency of the U.S. government set up in 1933 to pay back money you put in the bank if the bank defaults.

File: A place where you keep your tax and other financial records.

Financial Planner: Professional who helps you plan and reach your financial goals.

Global Fund: A mutual fund that invests in companies in many foreign countries and in the United States.

Global Investment: Investing outside of the United States.

Goal: Something you want to achieve for yourself or someone you love.

Growth: When something you buy can be sold for a higher price.

Income: Money that comes to you from anyone in any way.

IRA (Individual Retirement Account): A retirement account where you can put in up to $2,000 per year and accumulate growth or interest on a tax-deferred basis.

Insurance Agent: One licensed to help you buy insurance.

Interest: Money that you are paid for lending your money to others or that you pay to others when you borrow money.

International Fund: A mutual fund that invests in companies in foreign countries.

Investing: (1) Using your money to buy something that will make more money for you when you sell it or (2) lending your money to others to get interest.

Kiddie Tax: A tax on the earnings from children's investments or earnings. Kids pay at their parents' rate until age fourteen, when they get their own tax bracket.

Lawyer: One licensed to practice law. In money matters, often helps in tax problems.

Lend: Let others borrow your money.

Long-term Goal: Something you want to achieve in the future.

Markup: The difference between what a bond costs a broker and what it is sold to you for.

Maturity Date: Date a loan must be paid back with interest.

Mutual Fund: A fund that owns lots of securities and pools the money of investors to buy them. It is operated by an investment company.

Plan: A strategy to achieve a goal.

Prospectus: A disclosure document telling the details of the mutual fund that issues it.

Real Estate: Property such as a house or a store.

Real Estate Broker or Agent: One licensed to buy and sell real estate for you.

Securities: Stocks or bonds.

Shareholders' Meeting: Meeting between the people who own a particular stock and the company executives, usually to vote on matters of management. Takes place once a year.

Shares of Stock: Units of ownership in a company.

Short-term Goal: Something you want to achieve quickly.

Socially Responsible Investing: Investing in companies that have the same values that you have.

Tax: Money you pay to the national, state, or city government every year on your earnings.

Tax Deferred: Earnings that don't get taxed until the year in which you use the money.

Tax Exempt: Earnings that never get taxed.

Tax Free: Also earnings that never get taxed.

Unit: A share in a mutual fund.

Bibliography

Arthur's Funny Money. Lillian Hoban. New York: Harper & Row Publishers, 1981.

Bernard Baruch. Joanne Landers Henry. New York: Bobbs-Merrill, 1991.

Children and Money. Grace W. Weinstein. New York: New American Library, 1985.

Fast Cash for Kids. Bonny Drew. Hawthorne, N.J.: Career Press, 1991.

Finding Your First Job. Sue Alexander. New York: E.P. Dutton, 1980.

The First Official Money Making Book for Kids. Fred Shanaman. New York: Bantam Books, 1983.

From Workshop to Toy Store. Richard C. Levy and Ronald O. Weingartner. New York: Simon & Schuster, 1992.

How to Turn Lemons into Money: Money Basics. David Wallace. Englewood Cliffs, N.J.: Prentice-Hall, 1984.

How to Turn Up Into Down Into Up: A Child's Guide to Inflation, Depression, and Economic Recovery. Louise Armstrong. New York: Harcourt Brace Jovanovich, 1976.

Moneyskills. Bonny Drew. Hawthorne, N.J.: Career Press, 1992.

More Free Stuff for Kids. Elizabeth H. Weiss. Deephaven, Minn.: Meadowbrook Press, 1993.

United States Coin Collector's Check List. Racine, Wis.: Western Publishing Company, 1988.

Your Kids, Your Money. Adriane G. Berg. Englewood Cliffs, N.J.: Prentice-Hall, 1985.

Games

Ax Your Tax. Barbara Doyle Carlton Careers. Parker Brothers.

Hotels. Milton Bradley.

Interplay Rat Race. Waddingtons House of Games.

The Inventors. Parker Brothers.

Money Card. Schaper Manufacturing Company.

Power Barrons. Milton Bradley.

Rags to Riches. Computer Market Simulation Games.

$peculation. Cayla Games, Inc.

Trump the Game. Milton Bradley.

And the granddaddy of them all:
Monopoly. Parker Brothers.

College Books

Cash for College. Cynthia Ruiz McCee and Phillip C. McCee, Jr. New York: Hearst Books, 1993.

Free Money for College. Laurie Blum. New York: Facts on File, 1993.

The Scholarship Book. Daniel J. Cassidy and Michael J. Alves. Englewood Cliffs, N.J.: Prentice-Hall, 1990.

Index

Accountants, 82-83
Allowances, 106-8

Balancing a checkbook, 110-12
Bankers, 79-80
Banks
  FDIC insurance, 42
  loans from, 90
  using your money, 40-41
  withdrawal from, 42-43
Bear market, 53
Bills. *See* Paying bills
Bonds
  corporate bonds, 47
  markups, 81
  municipal bonds, 45–47, 121–22
  U.S. Savings Bonds, 39, 44–45,
    49–50
Borrowing money, 86
  bad borrowing, 92–94
  collateral, 88–89
  for college, 116–17, 118
  comparing interest rates, 89–90
  cost of, 87–89
  credit cards, 89, 90–91
  creditworthiness, 87–88, 93–94
  debt, 86
  default, 88, 93, 95
  for house buying, 94–96
  interest and, 86
  leveraged borrowing, 94–96
  line of credit, 87
  Marble-Borrowing Game, 86
  mortgage, 95
  places to borrow money, 89–90
  prime rate of interest, 88
  shopping for money, 89–90
Brokers, 60, 80–81, 83–84
  deep-discount brokers, 83
  discount brokers, 81, 83
  and DRIPs, 84
  real estate brokers, 82
Budget, 125
  and allowance, 107–8
  balancing of, 23–24
  family budget, 24
  form, 25
  income and expenses, 20–24
  lists, 27–29
  savings left over, 23, 24, 28
  for spenders and savers, 26–29
  things you can do without, 27–
    28, 29
  things you really want, 21–23
  types of budgets, 26–29
  what it is, 19–20
Bull market, 53

Capital, 36, 51
CDs, 42
CFPs, 82
Checking accounts, 110–12

Collateral, 88–89
Collectibles, 68–70
College costs, 114, 115–16
　don't be scared, 116
　loans and grants, 116–117, 118
　prepayment of tuition,117–18
　tips for getting to college, 116–18
Commissions to brokers, 80
Commodities, 68
Cost of living, 21
CPAs, 82–83
Credit. *See* Borrowing money
Credit cards, 89, 90–91
Currency conversion, 77–78

Default, 45–46, 88, 93, 95
Discount brokers, 81
Diversification, 63–64
Dividends, 52, 55–56
　reinvesting, 58–59
Dollar cost averaging, 64
DRIPs, 58–59, 84

Expansion, 7
Expenses, 21

Family discussion and exercises,
　131–33
FDIC insurance, 42
Federal Reserve Board (Fed), 5–6
Feelings about money, 124–27
Financial planners, 81–82
Foreign countries, 74–75
　ADRs (American Depository
　　Receipts), 75–76
　bonds on, 76
　currency investing, 77–78
　emerging growth countries, 75
　foreign income funds, 76
　international mutual funds, 75
　World of Money Game, 78

Games
　"All the Eggs in One Basket"
　　Game, 63
　Bull's-Eye Game, 41
　Heads and Tails Money Game, 9
　Leverage Game, 96–97
　Marble-Borrowing Game, 86
　Matching Game: Stock Stuff,
　　60–61
　Match the Professionals Game,
　　83
　Totally Awesome Risk/Reward
　　Game, 38–39
　World of Money Game, 78

Global investing, 74–78
Goals, 12, 124–25
　cheap and expensive goals, 13
　good things about them, 12–13
　long-term goals, 13, 14
　plan, making of, 13–17
　short-term goals, 13–14
　things to do, 18
　wish to goal via plan, 13–17
Gross national product (GNP), 9
Growth, 36, 51

Healthy economy, 8, 9
House buying, 94–96

Income, 20–21
Inflation, 35
Insurance salesman, 82
Interest, 31–32, 40, 42, 43,47
　and borrowing, 86
　compound interest, 48–49
　doubling your money, 49
　prime rate, 88
　on savings bonds, 45
　shopping for, 49–50

Investing, 36
 bonds. *See* Bonds
 buy today to sell for more
  tomorrow, 37, 51–57
 capital, 36
 CDs, 42
 collectibles, 68–70
 commodities, 68
 contests, 54
 currency investing, 77–78
 in foreign countries, 74–78
 global investing, 74–78
 growth, 36
 IRAs, 122
 lending money, 37, 41–50
 maturity date, 43
 mutual funds. *See* Mutual funds
 professional help in, 79–84
 reasons for, 34–35
 REITs, 68
 risk. *See* Risk
 rules for, 47
 socially responsible investing,
  71–73, 126
 speculation, 37
 stocks. *See* Stocks
 for tax savings, 121–22
 things to think about, 65–66
IRA (individual retirement
 account), 122
IRS (Internal Revenue Service),
 120, 121

Jobs and work, 100
 customer agreement, 101–2
 getting raises, 102–3
 looking for work, 101, 103–4
 parents and grandparents,
  first jobs of, 104–5
 things to try, 103–4
 tough on-the-job problems, 105-6

Knowledge of money
 growing up, 3
 what you already know, 2
 where it comes from, 4–11

Lawyers, 82
Leverage, 94–97
Lincoln, Abraham, 10

Making money
 getting or earning it, 6–7, 9–11.
  See also Jobs and work
 goals and plans, 13–17
 money making money. *See*
  Investing
Maturity date, 43, 45, 47
Mint, 4–5
Money making money. *See*
 Investing
Mortgage, 95
Municipal bonds, 45–47, 121–22
Mutual funds
 basics of, 62–63
 diversification, 63–64
 dollar cost averaging, 64
 foreign income funds, 76
 getting lists of, 65
 growth and income funds, 65
 international mutual funds, 75
 no-load funds, 65, 81
 prospectus, 63
 REIT, 68
 socially responsible, 72
 things to think about, 65–66
 unit share, 62

Newspapers, 54–56

Older kids
 college costs, 114, 115–18
 taxes, 119–23

Parents
  family discussion and exercises,
    131–33
  first jobs they had, 104
  things to ask them, 18, 104
Paying bills, 109–10
  bouncing a check, 112
  checkbook balancing, 110–12
P/E (price/earnings ratio), 53, 54,
    55, 56, 57
Plans, 13–17
Playing the market, 60
Prime rate, 88
Professional help, 79–84
Prospectus, 63

Quizzes, 14–16, 128–29

Real estate, 68, 70
  agents or brokers, 82
  REITs, 68
Real life and money
  allowances, 106–8
  jobs and work, 100–106
  paying bills, 100, 109–12
Recession, 7, 8
Recovery, 7
REIT, 68
Retirement, 34
Riddles, 43, 112
Risk, 35, 37–39, 47
  diversification, 63
  FDIC insurance, 42
  of stocks, 51, 52
Ruth, Babe, 11

Savings, 28
  after budget, 23, 24, 28
  day-of-deposit to day-of-
    withdrawal crediting, 32

how money grows, 31–32
interest rates, 31–32
putting money away, 31
waiting for things, 30
Savings bonds, 39, 44–45, 49–50
Sinetar, Marsha, 99
Socially responsible
  investing, 71–73, 126
Speculation, 37
Spend-and-save cards, 90–91
Stocks, 51, 80
  ADRs, 75–76
  bear market, 53
  brokers, 60, 80
  bull market, 53
  buying on margin, 94
  buying shares, 59–60
  checking on your stock, 54–56
  clubs to join, 57, 59
  commissions, 80
  dividends, 52, 55–56, 58–59
  dollar cost averaging, 64
  DRIPs, 58–59, 84
  in foreign companies, 75–76
  investing contests, 54
  in newspapers, 54–56
  P/E (price/earnings ratio), 53,
    54, 55, 56, 57
  picking stocks, 52–54
  playing the market, 60
  risk of, 51, 52
  round and odd lots of, 81
  tips from the author, 57
  undervalued stock, 60
  yield, 52–53, 56
Success, 16–17, 125–26, 131–33

Taxes, 119
  audit, 120
  collection system, 119–20

Taxes *(continued)*
  deductions, 121
  how much you'll pay, 120–21
  investing to save, 121–22
  IRAs, 122
  IRS, 120, 121
  kids tax, 122–23
  municipal bonds, 47, 121–22
  tax bracket, 120, 123
  tax deferral, 122
  what do you think, 126–27
Tests, 14–16, 128–29

U.S. Government
  debt of, 92
  money supply, 4–9

savings bonds, 39, 44–45, 49–50
  taxes, 119–23
Unit share, 62

Wall Street Journal, 54, 73
Where money comes from
  circulation of money, 8–9
  Fed, the, 5–6
  getting money (kids), 6–7, 9–11
  making coins and bills, 4–5
  supply of money, 4–9
Wishes and goals, 13–17
Withdrawal, 42–43
Work. *See* Jobs and work

Yield, 52–53, 56

More Newmarket Press Books for Kids (and Their Parents)

Adriane Berg on Money Management

Financial Planning for Couples: How to Work Together to Build Security and Success, Updated Edition—Berg shows couples of all incomes how to make money as a team. Her practical, 10-step money management program covers recordkeeping, budgeting, investment decisions, and much more.

Your Wealth-Building Years: Financial Planning for 18- to 38-Year-Olds, Second Edition—This invaluable handbook for young adults explains real estate, job bene-fits, financial instruments, and budgeting in addition to shared housing and socially responsible investing.

The Totally Awesome Business Book for Kids (and Their Parents)—Everything kids need to know about business. Includes illustrations, a bibliography, and a glossary.

The Totally Awesome Money Book for Kids (And Their Parents)—This fun, fact-filled guide uses quizzes, games, riddles, forms, charts, stories, and drawings to cover the basics of saving, investing, borrowing, working, and taxes.

Lynda Madaras on Growing Up

My Body, My Self for Boys: The "What's Happening to My Body?" Workbook for Boys
My Body, My Self for Girls: The "What's Happening to My Body?" Workbook for Girls
My Feelings, My Self: Lynda Madaras' Growing-Up Guide for Girls
*The "What's Happening to My Body?" Book for Boys: A Growing-Up Guide
  for Parents and Sons*
*The "What's Happening to My Body?" Book for Girls: A Growing-Up Guide
  for Parents and Daughters*

Order from your local bookstore or write to:
Newmarket Press, 18 E. 48th St., NY, NY 10017

Please send me:

____*Financial Planning* @ $10.95 (pb)

____*My Body, My Self for Girls* @ $11.95 (pb)

____*My Body, My Self for Boys* @ $11.95 (pb)

____*My Feelings, My Self* @ $11.95 (pb)

____*Money Book for Kids* @ $18.95 (hc)

____*Money Book for Kids* @ $10.95 (pb)

_____ *Business Book for Kids* @ $10.95 (pb)

_____ *"What's Happening?" for Boys* @ $ 18.95 (hc)

_____ *"What's Happening?" for Boys* @ $11.95 (pb)

_____ *"What's Happening?" for Girls* @ $18.95 (hc)

_____ *"What's Happening?" for Girls* @ $11.95 (pb)

_____ *Your Wealth-Building Years* @ $11.95 (pb)

For postage and handling, add $3.00 for the first book, plus $1.00 for each additional book. NY State residents should include appropriate sales tax. Allow 4–6 weeks for delivery. Prices and availability are subject to change.

I enclose check or money order payable to Newmarket Press in the amount of $ _____

NAME _____

ADDRESS _____

CITY/STATE/ZIP _____

For quotes on quantity purchases, or for a copy of our catalog, please write Special Sales, Newmarket Press, 18 E. 48th St., NY, NY 10017, call 212-832-3575, or fax 212-832-3629.

abergbob.qxd 9/24/97